WE DELIVER

A Chronicle of the Deeds
Performed by the Men and
Women of the U.S. Postal
Service

Tom Riley

HERITAGE BOOKS
2016

HERITAGE BOOKS

AN IMPRINT OF HERITAGE BOOKS, INC.

Books, CDs, and more—Worldwide

For our listing of thousands of titles see our website
at
www.HeritageBooks.com

Published 2016 by
HERITAGE BOOKS, INC.
Publishing Division
5810 Ruatan Street
Berwyn Heights, Md. 20740

International Standard Book Numbers
Paperbound: 978-0-7884-5713-5
Clothbound: 978-0-7884-6423-2

This book is dedicated to my wife Crucy and to my two wonderful daughters, Gina and Bernadette. To my friend, Dr. Tom Nardi and to all the men and women who serve in our armed forces in Iraq and Afghanistan. And to my grandson, Benjamin Noah Riley, a future golf professional.

Table of Contents

Preface

This book is a tribute to the 790,000 men and women who comprise the number of people employed by the U.S. Postal Service. It is especially dedicated to the hard working letter carriers past and present who perform their tasks in all kinds of weather, and under a workload that doubles every 20 years. The U.S. Postal Service delivers 40% of the World's Mail, often under severe budget constraints and the criticism of those few who would privatize the U.S. Postal Service.

As a letter carrier for 27 years, I was struck by the varied interest, hobbies and volunteer efforts of many of the carriers. A portion of this book is devoted to those men and women who saw a need in their communities and who unselfishly responded to it. There are stories about courage and kindness, heroism and humor, some of the qualities I have noted in Carriers both here in Nanuet and elsewhere as they go about delivering mail throughout the United States.

As the only government representative who has daily contact with the public, the letter carrier is in a position to appreciate the problems and needs of the constituents faced as they go about their daily rounds. A survey of readers taken by *U.S.A TODAY* on the very day the price of stamps was raised to 39 cents revealed that 82% of the general public believes the U.S. Postal Service is doing a good job. As a recently retired carrier, I can attest to the fact that every effort is being made to do an even better job.

Letter carriers throughout the United States, exemplified by the deeds recounted in this book, can face the future with all its problems and opportunities. Letter carriers and the employees who work for the United States Postal Service have met the challenges imposed by modern society and some have performed beyond the call of duty.

My thanks to Vince Sombrotto, President of the National Association of Letter Carriers, for permission to reprint articles that appeared in *THE POSTAL RECORD*, a monthly publication of the NALC. Thanks and appreciation are extended to Rita L. Moroney, Research Administrator/Historian for using information obtained in her fine book, *HISTORY OF THE U.S. POSTAL SERVICE—1775-1984*. Acknowledgement and thanks are extended to Pat McCabe, General Manager of the Library Division of the U.S. Postal Service in Washington D.C. for many of the photographs appearing in this book, and to Scott H. Bell of the NALC's Communication Department for use of photographs in stories reprinted from *THE POSTAL RECORD*.

The early history of the postal service worldwide was obtained from the *Encyclopedia Britanica*, Volume 25 of the 15th Edition-1987 and the *GUINNESS BOOK OF STAMPS, FACTS AND FEATS* by James MacKay. The Profile of Postmaster General Anthony M. Frank appeared in the Spring 1988 edition of *POSTAL LIFE*, a magazine for postal employees and their families. William R. Cummings, Regional Postmaster is to be thanked for allowing me to reprint portions of an article dealing with automation that appeared in the *NORTHEAST REGIONAL BULLETIN.*

I would like to thank Lorraine Swerdloff, Director of Communications for *THE POSTAL RECORD* and her staff for allowing me to reprint articles from *THE POSTAL RECORD*. A portion of the proceeds from this book will be donated to the Postal Relief Fund to aid victims of natural disasters such as Hurricane Hugo and the San Francisco earthquake.

I would like to thank Margot A. Myers, Regional Communications Administrator, Northeast Regional Office and *RESOURCE MAGAZINE* for information on Automation.

Thanks to *THE NATIONAL GEOGRAPHIC SOCIETY* for allowing me to reprint an article on the Pony Express. Thanks is given to Temple University Press for the reprint of excerpts from *Democratic Vistas: Post Offices and Public Art in the New Deal* by Marlene Parks and Gerald Markowitz. ABC News, *Nightline* is also to be thanked for allowing me to quote excerpts from their program on March 16th 1990.

I would like to thank H.E. Harris & Company, Portmouth, New Hampshire for allowing me to reprint material from *AMAZING BUT TRUE STORIES BEHIND THE STAMPS* by Doug Storer. Rita L. Moroney, Research Administrator/Historian of the United States Postal Service is to be credited for supplying me with material for the Postal Lore and Trivia section and for information on the early history of postal services in the U.S. Thanks is also given to former Postmaster General Benjamin F. Bailar who recounted the history of the Postal Service in a speech he gave at Monmouth College, Monmouth, Illinois on October 16, 1975.

I would like to thank the *Federal Times* of Springfield, Virginia for granting me permission to reprint articles *"Remembering '70: Workers Risk It All In Historic Strike "* and *"Inspectors' Crime Labs Mark 50th Anniversary"* from their newspaper. Special thanks is given to Paul M. Griffo, Senior Information Specialist of the Postal Inspection Service for his invaluable help in obtaining information about our Postal Inspection Service. I would like to thank Brian Fitzpatrick, MSC Director of Marketing and Communication for the Mid-Hudson MSC for his support.

Writing a book and making the rounds necessary to publicize it sometimes takes hard work when one is working full-time. With all the demands of family life and other distractions I would like to thank all those who aided me in one form or another especially Laura Incalcaterra, editor of *ROCKLAND REVIEW*, a community newspaper for her long and kind article on *WE DELIVER*.

Chapter I

The importance of mail delivery on a regular basis is often taken for granted by the citizens of the United States. It took a crisis of unusual dimension to point out the great human need for sustained communication over long distances. When American troops were deployed in Saudi Arabia during Operation Desert Shield their hunger for news from worried parents, friends and relatives brought about one of the largest recorded outpouring of letters, parcels, books, and gifts to the brave men and women serving in our armed forces there.

School children all over the United States wrote letters, sent gifts and reassured these soldiers that they were not forgotten and that they were very much appreciated. These letters, gifts, books and parcels buoyed up our troops and kept morale high in a lonely desert, thousands of miles from home. Soldiers realized that strangers they had never seen were touched by their bravery and the sacrifice they had made in serving their country.

In the March 1991 issue of *THE POSTAL RECORD*, a publication of the National Association of Letter Carriers a report from the front showed how important mail was to the soldiers shouldering the burden of war.

Military Postal Units Are a Vital Link
Between the Troops and the Home Front

These days when Larry Bevis delivers the mail, he surrounded by a sea of sand and soldiers hungry for letters from their love ones thousands of miles away. Bevis and three other Florence, Alabama Branch 892 members-Kenneth Frost, William Childers and Doug Pate are part of Army Reserve 336th Postal Unit, trained to move the mail to U.S. troops at war. Called up the day after Christmas, the four letter carriers said a hasty goodbye to friends and loved ones and were soon in Saudi Arabia.

There they helped move the more than 325,000 pounds of mail our troops in the Persian Gulf received each day. "I've been in the postal business for 23 years," said Bevis, 43, "and I've never seen anything like this." To keep up with the mail flow, the Branch 892 members worked 12-hour shifts, seven days a week. Huge containers airlifted to Dharhan, Saudi Arabia contained sacks of mail that were broken open, sorted by platoon, and dispatched to a designated mail clerk within each unit-a challenge for units on the move in hostile territory. Then with his or her comrades gathered anxiously around, the roll call began, and the soldiers once again renewed their links to loved ones back home.

The need for a system to exchange written communication has been felt by all societies. This very basic need to communicate over long distances marks the advent of postal services. *WE DELIVER* is a history and study of the postal system and the people who work for it. As a letter carrier for twenty seven years I have had the opportunity to view many aspects of its operation and to come in contact on a daily basis with some of the hardest working people I have ever met.

Their performance in handling the hundreds of millions of letters, parcels, and gifts to American troops stationed in the Persian Gulf along with millions of other letters heading overseas was handled with relative ease. As it has been during every crisis where American troops are involved, Americans, like people everywhere, love to receive mail from the home front. Soldiers can tell how much a heartfelt letter from home lifts their spirit and morale.

Communication, the lifeblood of every society has undergone tremendous advances over the centuries. One of the earliest messages as recorded in the Old Testament of the Bible was transported by a dove to Noah in the form of an olive branch. Moses inscribed the Ten Commandments in stone tablets to stress their importance and to etch into the memory of his people lasting principles of human conduct. From these etchings into a stone tablet to the transfer of electronic mail via satellite a long, difficult process has taken place. As speedier means of transporting letters were devised so did the demand for postal services increased. The basic function of postal organizations is to turn that letter that you mail and place in a collection box into something that can be handled on a bulk basis, so that eventually it can regain its individual status. That is what happens when my daughter, Bernadette who lives in New City, N.Y. wants to communicate with her friend, Rachel who lives in Ellicott City, Maryland. She places her letter in the mailbox where it is collected by our mail carrier, Frank as he delivers our mail. Upon completion of his route he adds Bernadette's letter to thousands of other letters being sent to the Maryland region of our country. At that point postal clerks insure that it regains its individual status and arrives at Rachel's house in Ellicott City, Maryland. In 1995 the total mail volume reached 181 billion pieces.

Good communication was essential for governing the vast empires of the ancient world. Soldiers serving in Operation Desert Shield and now in Bosnia already appreciative of regular mail delivery would be interested to know that the Persian Gulf region was the birthplace of postal services around 3,500 B.C. In Persia the King pressed his ring into a clay tablet where a message had been inscribe. The tablet was set out in the hot desert sun to dry. Once dried, mounted couriers delivered these heavy letters. A treasure trove of these heavy letters was discovered in the early 1900's in a cave in Turkey. They offer a vivid account of business transactions and court life of that era.

The Egyptians had a unique way of transmitting messages. Around 4,000 B.C. the rulers of Egypt had one their slaves head shaved and inscribed a message on his bald head. He was held in captivity until his hair grew back. He was then sent on his way. If he became apprehended while passing through enemy lines he could rightly claim no knowledge of the message. The intended receiver of the message would shave the slaves' head to read the King's decrees. Many centuries later the extensive use of papyrus for messages and record-keeping by Egyptian court officials popularized the use of lightweight material for transmitting messages.

The Chinese developed a Post House relay system that is credited as the world's first Postal Service. Under the Chou Dynasty, 1000 B.C. mounted couriers delivered messages on paper, which was invented by the Chinese. These couriers delivered the Emperor's decrees to far-flung villages and provinces. The postal service was not for public use and anyone caught using it for their own use did so under penalty of death, if apprehended. The relay system was brought to a high state of development under the Mongol Emperors. In the 13th Century Marco Polo remarked that the Post House relay system reached every corner of the Empire with over 25,000 stations.

Herodotus, the Greek historian described his admiration for the Post House relay system of Cyrus, the Great of Persia in the 6th Century B.C. Those remarks are etched in stone across the facade of the Manhattan General Post Office on 34th Street. "Neither snow, nor rain, nor gloom of night shall stop these carriers from the full completion of their appointed rounds." These words readily come to the mind of New Yorkers as they see mail carriers enter their shops to deliver the mail in all kinds of weather. Herodotus's words are as timely today as they were 25 hundred years ago.

It was the development of Rome from a small city state into a vast empire that ushered in the most highly developed postal system of the ancient world. The Roman Empire with its ability to construct a vast network of roads to unite its far-flung provinces created in turn a need to communicate with them. The Cursus Publicus or Roman Post Office was established at convenient interval along the great roads of the Empire. The Cursus Publicus served the political and military needs of the empire for a speedy and reliable system of communication between Rome and its many provinces.

Chariots were used to carry the mail, often holding over 400 pounds of letters. An inspectorial system to oversee the operation and prevent abuses was similar in nature to our own Postal Inspection Service. The Cursus Publicus was highly organized and the speed at which it could deliver messages was not to be rivaled until the 19th Century.

After the fall of the Roman Empire in the west, the political fragmentation of Europe caused all traces of the Roman Postal System to disappear. Although the barbarian rulers admired the Cursus Publicus and tried to keep it intact, communities bordering the great roads refused to maintain them and they fell into disarray. The lack of a central administration in Rome and the political disintegration of the times broke apart the Cursus Publicus.

In the Americas, the pre-Columbian civilizations felt the same need to communicate. The Mayans developed a road network for foot messengers that lasted 1,000 years. The Incas also developed means to communicate over long distances by relay systems. American Indians developed a rudimentary parcel post system to transfer fresh catches of fish and game to their villages by means of foot messengers.

Chapter II

The ingenuity of man in devising means to communicate over distances is a tribute to man's imagination. He has at various times used pigeons, reindeer, rockets, kites, balloons, cats, arrows, catapults, camels, sea currents, tin cans, gliders, horses, zinc-coated steel balls, dogs, airplanes, cars, trucks, and railroads. As faster means of transportation were devised the postal service was quick to make use of them. Electronic mail delivery using satellites to aid delivery is the most modern example of man's quest to communicate as rapidly as possible.

Our world has grown smaller due to faster communications and rapid travel. The great differences in cultures and languages are minimized somewhat by the diverse transmission of knowledge through mail and the electronic media. Man is constantly striving to broaden his horizons. Prejudice and ignorance diminish as each person realizes he is a member of the global community of man.

Mail has fostered bonds of friendship and opened doors of opportunity to millions of people. The immigrant to the U.S. from Africa is connected to his native country by the bonds of his weekly correspondence with family back home. Business opportunities are spotted and relayed so commerce is enlarged between countries. The expansion of the European Economic Community will result in greater correspondence and increased demands on postal services. Information is power and the transmission of mail throughout the global community will improve as the 21st Century unfolds.

The Greek philosopher, Theophrastus launched bottles containing messages into the Mediterranean. He wanted to prove that the Mediterranean fed into the Atlantic Ocean. Sea currents took his bottles into the Atlantic where mariners recovered his bottles and proved his theory.

Probably the first airborne letter was sent on an arrow during a siege of an embattlement long before the birth of Christ. We know that the first airborne message to man was sent to Noah by a dove bearing an olive branch. That message of hope to a besieged humanity proved God's love for all living things.

Pigeons have a long history in aiding man in his desire to communicate. Ancient Greeks, Hebrews, Chinese and Persians often used pigeons during sieges. Pigeons wounded in flight have been known to walk home. With the development of microfilm the importance of pigeons magnified. During a siege of Paris in 1871 microfilm was inserted into goose quills that were tied to the pigeon's tail feathers. Over 30,000 letters could be sent this way on one pigeon.

The Chinese used kites to transport messages during a siege in the 6th Century A.D. The English used balloons in the late 1700's to drop letters overboard. As faster, more efficient means of transportation were devised so man used it to communicate. Dogs, cats, camels and reindeer were used at various times until technology improved to the point where steamships, railroads and airplanes aided communications. Now computers, satellites and fax machines provide even faster means to communicate.

It was during the Industrial Revolution that the demand for better mail service to serve the growing commercial and manufacturing centers took place. The improved roads of London and the development of the stagecoach speeded up the delivery of mail. Letters could be delivered the morning after posting in towns 120 miles from London.

Rowland Hill's Reforms

In 1837, a British educator and tax reformer, Rowland Hill published *POST OFFICE REFORM: IT'S IMPORTANCE AND PRACTICABILITY*. It is regarded as a milestone in postal progress. He studied the cost structure of postal operations and came to the conclusion that conveyance charges were not an important factor in the total cost of mailing a letter. He realized that the current intricate charging scales based on distance were irrelevant. He also showed how the collection of money payment was easily avoidable. Hill's solution was a uniform rate of postage regardless of distance using prepaid adhesive stamps sold by the post office.

Hill's proposals gained strong support. His one penny for each half ounce of mail found favor with the general public. The "Penny Post" was introduced in 1840 and was an instant success because it brought postal services to the masses.

Today, the modern postal service is indebted to Hill's reforms. They are the key to the speed and delivery with which the modern postal system handles billions of letters daily. The reduced rate of postage for printed matter helped the spread of education.

The development of the railroad speeded up the delivery of mail. Letters were sorted in transit and delivered the day after at distances 3 to 4 times as great as had been possible with the stagecoach. By the end of the 19th Century, Britain, Europe and the U.S. and India had built up a complex network of rail service.

International Postal Reform: The Universal Postal Union. Postal relations between countries were composed of a bewildering variety of currencies and units of weight and measurements. Postal treaties worked out between countries became so complex that they interfered with the free exchange of international mail. Something had to be done.

The first practical steps toward reform took place in May 1863 when delegates of 15 European and American postal administrators met at the Paris Postal Conference which was convened at the suggestion of the United States. The conference established important general principles for the simplification of procedures, which were adopted as a model by the countries concerned.

The American Civil War delayed a formal international treaty. On September 15th the International Postal Congress met in Bern, Switzerland. It was attended by representatives of 22 states. On October 9th, 1874 a *"Treaty concerning the Establishment of a General Postal Union"* was signed. The treaty provides a uniform framework of rules and procedures for the exchange of international mail. The Union grew rapidly. By 1914 when China was admitted it included almost all independent countries. Since 1948 the U.P.U has been a specialized agency of the United Nation.

Postal Services today still rely on carriers and clerks to mediate the delivery of mail. The use of automation and optical readers keep the price of mailing a letter cost-effective. In 1875 it cost $5.00 to mail a letter from Missouri to San Francisco via Pony Express. Today it cost only 39 cents to mail a letter twice that distance. The Postal Service in the U.S. is still the most cost-effective in terms of mail delivery among the industrialized nations of the world. The progressive use of automation and human resources has enabled the U.S. to keep the cost of postage low compared to the rest of the industrialized world.

As the U.S. Postal Service approaches the 21st century quality control and employee participation in management decisions are expected to improve service and reduce the error rate. Automation will speed the delivery of an ever increasing volume of mail as attrition in the total number of people employed by the U.S. Postal Service will help it to maintain its status as the most cost efficient deliverer of the world's mail.

Chapter III

The "father of the U.S. Postal Service," Benjamin Franklin was appointed Postmaster General of the United States by the Second Continental Congress on July 26, 1775. His postal achievements were a small part of the contributions this man made to his era. His accomplishments as a printer, publisher, philosopher, philanthropist and statesman made him a legend even in his own time. He received a salary of $1,000 a year.

A hundred years earlier Richard Fairbank's Tavern in Boston was designated the official repository for mail brought or sent overseas. Coffee houses and taverns were used by other civilized nations as mail drops. 50 years earlier Governor Lovelace of New York set up a monthly post between N.Y. and Boston using the Old Boston Post Road which is presently U.S. Route 1.

Central Postal organization came to the colonies in 1691 when Thomas Neale received a 21 year grant from the British Crown for a North American Postal Service. Neale never came to America; although his franchise cost 80 cents a year, he died heavily in debt.

Deputy Postmaster General Alexander Spotswood appointed Ben Franklin as Postmaster General of Philadelphia in 1727. As Joint Postmaster General for the Crown, Franklin made many improvements. Surveys were made and shorter routes were set up. He reported his first surplus to the British Crown. He improved postal operations from Maine to Florida and mail operated on a regular schedule. While postmaster of Philadelphia, Franklin formed the city's first volunteer fire company. He also organized America's first hospital and started an academy that later became the University of Pennsylvania. As an inventor, Franklin had few peers. He invented the lightning rod, bifocal glasses, the copper-plate press to print paper money and the "Franklin Stove," which served for decades as the major heating unit for Americans.

Franklin became associated with changes that have had a lasting impact on the postal system. He designed distribution cases containing pigeon-holes for the deposit of mail for common destinations. He also improved the post roads by setting milestones (stone markers) along them. There was a sound reason for postmen to know how far they traveled to deliver the mail-they were paid by the distance they traveled, 3 pence a mile in summer and 3 1/2 pence in the winter.

The colonists were suspicious of the Royal Post and Franklin was dismissed by the Crown. After the Boston riots of 1774 Franklin was reappointed by the Continental Congress. America's present system descends in an unbroken line from Franklin's planned operation. As late as 1780 the Postal System consisted of 1 Postmaster General, 3 surveyors and 26 post riders. Philadelphia was the seat of government. When the Post Office Department moved to Washington D.C. in 1800 officials were able to carry all postal records, furniture and supplies in 2 wagons.

The Postal Inspection Service—the law enforcement arm of the Postal Service—also traces its lineage to Franklin, who as postmaster at Philadelphia was assigned the additional duties of "regulating the several post offices and bringing the postmasters to account." As a joint Postmaster General of the Colonies he continued these extra duties. When Franklin died on April 17, 1790 in Philadelphia, he was accorded one of the largest funerals the city had ever seen.

Railway Mail Service

Passage of the Act of July 1838 made all railroads in the U.S. post routes. Mail intended for local points was sorted and dropped off at local stops. By 1930 10,000 trains were being used to deliver mail to every hamlet in the U.S. By 1970 virtually all railroads were eliminated as mail transporters.

The Civil War

Street boxes for mail collection began to appear in big cities by 1858. In 1863 free city delivery was instituted in 49 of the country's largest cities. These and many other innovations were introduced by Postmaster General Montgomery Blair. Blair served during the critical Civil War years under President Lincoln. During the war, Blair had to meet unprecedented demands on mail service. A small rural post office would suddenly find itself deluged by thousands of soldiers and pieces of mail. Blair worked out a plan which gave every regiment its own postmaster.

He introduced other major changes. He discontinued unnecessary post offices. He made sure mail contracts were granted to the lowest bidder. By 1863, Blair had reduced the 1860 deficit of over $5.7 million to only $120,000. When he resigned in 1864, the Department was almost self-sustaining: It showed a surplus of $161,000 a year later.

Another of Blair's achievements was initiation of an international conference on postal problems. This meeting led to formation of the Universal Postal Union, which is still a model of quiet and effective international cooperation to deliver mail among nations, even between those involved in war with each other. Blair also introduced the concept of the railway post office, a railroad car in which mail is sorted and distributed en route.

In 1889 President Benjamin Harrison appointed John Wanamaker Postmaster General. Wanamaker was a Philadelphia merchant and a warm friend of the President. Wanamaker believed that the Post Office Department could be operated like a business-just as his store was. Many of the reforms he instituted were a harbinger of the postal reform enacted nearly a century later in 1971. Wanamaker claimed that the post office was not properly organized or managed. He showed great concern for postal employees, and they in turn were very impressed with him. Long after he retired they continued to visit him at his home and write to him.

Wanamaker's spirit and zeal as a merchant was transferred to his postal job. He emphasized a postal building program and services to the customer. He initiated house letter boxes and many other innovations. Wanamaker, however was not popular with Congress and that help to sink many of his programs. In later years, his ideas for rural free delivery, parcel post, and postal savings were enacted, but by then Wanamaker was no longer connected to the post office.

By 1880, 454 post offices were delivering mail to residents of U.S. cities. It was in 1900 that free delivery came to farmers and other rural residents. Before that people had to go to the post office to pick up their mail. If they refused a letter the post office labor and delivery costs were never recovered.

It is difficult for us to imagine the isolation and loneliness of the American farmer. On the way into town to pick up supplies he'd stop at the post office, sometimes he delayed and it was weeks or months before the mail was picked up. West Virginia was the first state to experiment with rural free delivery. Critics complained it was too costly and impractical to have a mailman trudge over rutted roads and through forest trying to deliver the mail in all kinds of weather.

The farmers were delighted and a new world opened up for them. One farmer estimated that in 15 years he had traveled 12,000 miles going to and from the post office to get the mail. A by-product of rural free delivery was the stimulation it provided to the development of the great American road system of roads and highways. A prerequisite for rural delivery is good roads. In one community in Indiana the farmers paid $2,600 to pave and gravel roads in order to qualify for rural free delivery. $72 million dollars was spent by towns on bridges, culverts and other improvements to qualify for rural free delivery.

Parcel Post

Rural free delivery increased the demand for delivery of small packages such as foodstuff, drugs, tobacco, and dry goods. Parcel Post became law in 1912. It was an instant success. Marketing and merchandising through Parcel Post gave rise to the great mail order houses that still exist.

Montgomery Ward, the 1st mail order house mailed out a one page catalogue in 1872. When parcel post became law, the mail

order catalogue became the most important book in the farm
house next to the Bible. It was often referred to as "the
Homesteader's Bible." Sears and Roebuck tripled its revenue
after Parcel Post. It bragged it was "selling a watch and four suits
every ten minutes, and a revolver every two minutes."

Air Mail

The U.S. Government was slow to recognize the potential of
the airplane. In 1905 the War Department refused 3 separate
offers by the Wright Brothers to share their scientific discovery on
air flight. By 1908, America owned only one dilapidated plane.

The Post Office, however, was intrigued with the possibility of
carrying mail through the skies. It authorized experimental mail
flights. Earl Ovington, sworn in as a mail carrier made daily
flights between Garden City and Mineola, Long Island dropping
his mail bags from the plane where the Mineola postmaster
picked them up. The post office urged the Army Signal Corp to
lend planes and pilots, arguing that it was good training for
student pilots. On August 1918 the Post Office hired its own pilots
and had planes specially built to carry mail. Beginning on
February 22, 1921 mail was flown both day and night from San
Francisco to New York. Three months later Congress
appropriated $1,250,000 for airmail expansion.

These early planes had no instruments, radios or other
navigational aids. Pilots flew by dead reckoning or by "the seat of
their pants." Fatalities were rare because of the slow landing
speed of the planes. By 1926 commercial airlines took over air
mail delivery.

The Pony Express

The Pony Express is memorable to adults and children alike because it romanticized the rough and tumble days of the settling of the American West. The lonely post rider outrunning Indian attacks to deliver the mail represented an example of the courage and daring needed to settle the wild West. Rowe Findley wrote an article in the July 1980 *NATIONAL GEOGRAPHIC* magazine that tells the story of that era.

"Here he comes!"

Away across the endless dead level of the prairie a black speck appears against the sky... sweeping toward us nearer and nearer...a whoop and a wave of the hand... and the man and his horse burst past our view and goes winging into the distance."

Mark Twain from a westbound stage beheld a Pony Express rider and so the rider has galloped into history, hat brim bent by the wind, dust flying from the staccato beat of dust digging hoof-beats. The pony express looms larger than truth, a buckeroo stew of fact and legend. The pony express rider risked death daily as Indian wars flamed across hundreds of miles of Utah territory, destroying relay stations, stock and 17 lives, including one to three riders depending on whose facts you accept. The bravest death is credited to an orphan, age 14.

William F Cody earned his spurs as a pony express rider at 15. He earned his nickname "Wild Bill" in a controversial shoot out while in the employ of the Pony Express. Another spunky lad, Elijah "Nick" Wilson survived a barbed arrow in his skull and so inspired dime store novelist Ned Buntline, who wrote about his hair-raising adventures.

The true facts are that the pony express rider averaged ten miles an hour. In darkness or uphill he slowed for safety or to spare his mount and he usually arrived on time with the mail and scalp intact. The Pony Express lasted only 18 months and grew out of a long frustrated need. By 1860 almost half a million Americans lived west of the Rocky Mountains, most of them in California and Oregon. They were lured there by the opportunity for land and gold and they were concerned for news from home, those settled states east of the Missouri River.

The freighting firm of Russell, Majors and Wadell already possessed of 55 acres of corralled horses decided they had a head start as they were running a stage line to all the U.S. Army posts in the West. Most of the horses were western mustangs, good for fast getaways from Indians.

The Pony Express began in St. Joseph, Missouri, the western end of the nation's railroads in 1860 and ended at the Sacramento quay where the mail was flung aboard a side-steamer for San Francisco. Several months after it began the Paiutes, numbering perhaps 8,000 men, rose in a holy war to chase the white man from what is today most of Nevada and a slice of Utah. War parties attacked ranches and many Pony Express Stations came under attack, 17 employees were killed. One rider, Nick Wilson remembered fighting off the Indians for three days. He was struck by an arrow just above the eye. His friends pulled the arrow out but the flint spike remained embedded in his skull. His friends thought he was a goner. They abandoned him but came back the next day to bury him. They found him still alive. He remained in a coma for 18 days but recovered.

Billy Tate, only 14 was carrying the mail near Ruby Valley when a dozen braves rode him down in a desperate stand behind a rock. Friends later found him, pierced by many arrows, with seven of his attackers dead before him. The slain Billy still had his scalp, a sign that the warriors respected his courage.

Billy Cody, fatherless with a mother and sister in need hired on as a Pony Express rider at 15. Cody once rode 322 miles to deliver the mail when several riders were killed by Indians.

Mark Twain recounted a meeting with "Jack" Slade, Bill Cody's boss and Pony Express division chief. Slade, the reputed killer of 26 men sat at a table with Twain. Twain remarked: "I found myself at a table with "the actual orgre" but also found him "so friendly and so gentle-spoken that I warmed to him in spite of his awful history… the coffee ran out. At least it was reduced to one tin cupful, and Slade was about to take it when he saw my cup was empty. He politely offered to fill it, but…I politely declined. I was afraid he had not killed anybody that morning, and might be needing diversion…But nothing of the kind occurred. We left him with only twenty six dead people to account for…

It was the telegraph that put the Pony Express out of business. The telegraph project was a race by crews building east and west to see who could get to Salt Lake City first. The Missouri crew under Edward Creighton got there October 18th, 1861, the Californians under James Gamble six days later. The first message eastward assured President Lincoln of California's loyalty to the Union. In mere minutes it dot-dashed across the same route the Pony Express had ridden. In eighteen and a half months, by most estimates the enterprise lost some $200,000.

Chapter IV

The U.S. Post Office Undergoes an Era of Change

The following information is excerpted from the *"History of the U.S. Postal Service 1775-1984"* by Rita L. Moroney, Research Administrator/Historian.

The social correspondence of the earlier century gave way, gradually at first, then explosively, to business mail, until in 1963 business mail constituted 80% of the total volume. The largest impetus to this great outpouring was the result of the computer. Something had to be done. The introduction of the zip code and the development of 552 sectional centers, each serving 40 to 150 post offices allowed the post office to handle the record volume.

The zip code designates a broad geographical area of the U.S. This is followed by two digits which more closely pinpoints population concentrations. The final two digits designate small post offices or postal zones in larger zoned cities. A number of books have been written by a businessman who uses zip codes to aid businesses market their products in areas of zip codes where they are guaranteed to sell well.

In 1966, the Chicago Post Office ground to a virtual stop under a log jam of mail. The case for postal reform was summarized by Postmaster General Lawrence F. O'Brian. "We have no control over our work load, over the rates and revenue, over the pay rates for employees, over the conditions of the service of these employees and limited control over the transportation facilities we are compelled to use."

On August 12th, 1970 President Nixon signed the Postal Reorganization Act of 1970, providing for the conversion of the Post Office Department to the U.S. Postal Service, an independent establishment within the executive branch of the government.

Major Accomplishments Under Reorganization

A)   Streamlined the internal management using a Sectional, district, regional and Headquarters chain of command.

B)   Abolished patronage, now a merit system.

C)   Labor contracts achieved through collective bargaining.

D)   Developed programs for higher efficiency, faster service and economical handling of mail. (ie-Express Mail)

E)   Computerized forwarding.

F)   Presort First class-offer discount.

G)   Carrier Route-2nd class-discount for presorted.

H)   Consumer Advocate to handle complaints.

I)   Stream lined insurance claims to speed settlements.

J)   Use of color labels to reduce misrouting.

K)   Stamps by mail program.

L)   Increased money order denominations

M)   Accept Passport Applications in 1,000 locations

N)   Issue Food Stamps where there is a critical need

O)   Keep postage rates among the lowest in the industrialized world

P)   Devised Carrier Alert Program which has saved many lives. The carrier is alerted to a possible need for assistance by accumulated mail build-up.

Q)   Modernize and mechanized physical plants. 80% being sorted mechanically now, 25% before reorganization.

R)   Increase in gross productivity every year.

S)   Implementation of Employee Involvement to provide opportunities for employees to become involved in the identification and solution of problems which affect their work and the quality of their lives.

T)   Increasing emphasis on the need for equal employment opportunities and sensitivity toward minorities. Enforce all affirmative action programs.

U)   Employing one of the largest veteran and handicapped work force in the nation. About 50% of the work force is veterans.

V)   Inaugurating a Women's Program to insure equality of opportunity in the Post Office.

W)   Expanded Training Program at W.F. Bolger Management Academy and the Technical Training Center in Norman, Oklahoma.

X)   Expanded alcohol and drug awareness programs.

Y)   Crack down on Postal violators, pornographers, burglary losses, mail fraud. Over 200,000 cases investigated by postal inspectors and the Crime Lab.

Z)   Instituted an Energy Conservation Program in 18,000 facilities through in-house modification of the electrical and heating plant.

a)   Purchase of fuel efficient Long Life Vehicles which have a life expectancy of 24 years, compared to 8. The Post Office runs the 2nd largest operational fleet in the Western World. If the Post Office were considered a non-government business, it would be classified the 2nd largest employer and the 2nd largest retail business and the largest transportation-related company in the nation.

b)   Computerized information to track and monitor energy consumption.

c)   Utilized solar heating for space heating and hot water systems.

d)   Automated Window Services with the use of calculat9rs and computers into an integrated Retail Service Terminal. Expanded lobby hours to better service 9 to 5 jobs.

WE DELIVER

Democratic Vistas

Post Offices and Public Art in the New Deal
by Marlene Parks and Gerald E. Markowitz

Between 1934 and 1943 the Treasury Department's Section of Painting and Sculpture commissioned art work for over 1,100 Post Offices across the country. During the distressed times of the 1930's and the Depression, the New Deal took a protective role in providing art for the masses. The common man was upheld and found a protector in Franklin Roosevelt. The New Deal broadened the concept of democracy and based it on the economic sphere.

The government commissioned over 10,000 artists, many virtually unknown, some famous but most in desperate need of work. They produced a staggering amount of work, 100,000 easel paintings, 18,000 sculptures, 13,000 prints and more than 4,000 murals. This public art expressed the ideals fulfilled and unfulfilled of that era. It was an art of collaboration between the community, the people and government and the artist.

The leaders of the Section were Harry Hopkins and Frances Perkins who came from a social work background. All the Section leaders had a background in art. Edward Bruce, Edward Rowan and Forbes Watson headed the Section. Grant Wood, Leon Kroll, Henry Varnum Poor, Thomas Hart Benton were some of the muralist. National competitions were held to determine the artist. Local artist by and large prevailed and were preferred by the community. Most of the art was well received, some caused controversy.

After school many children gathered at the post offices to see works of art in progress. Many parents inquired about art education for their children. Some murals were the pride of the valley. Townspeople enjoyed seeing themselves in the paintings. The cold office walls of many post offices were warmed into life by fine painting and murals.

Most murals adopted themes that stressed continuity with a progressive and prosperous past and provided reassurance. But some were daring and dealt with strife and violence. Labor strikes and racial oppression occurred in some themes. Most themes dealt with the family as a source of strength and stability. Rural Free Delivery was depicted and celebrated in many of the murals. Free delivery of mail was accepted as one of the inalienable privileges of citizenship.

Many of the themes such as TVA, Introduction of Electricity, Erosion, Reforestation, etc, provided reassurance of an American ethic that was communal rather than individualistic. A mural over a Postmaster's door seems quaint anachronism today. Murals project a basic belief in the dignity of the people and their right to social justice and useful work. Art, once the province of the elite would now serve the people. Many artists painted the canvas in their studio and affixed them to a wall while others worked under conditions less than ideal, working around windows and lighting fixtures and clocks. Some artists were really creative. In a mural about early papermaking one artist placed the apparent weight of the press directly on top of the doorway, which appeared to be supporting the press.

Post offices today are the only environment in which one can view the diversity of representational styles that America enjoyed in the 1930's. It was an attempt to elevate the ordinary and give it new meaning. It was true to the widespread belief that progress, based on work, the efforts and faith of the people would win out. It made original art more widely available. It involved the local citizen in the decision-making. It responded to community vested interest. It employed many artists. It made every effort to ensure that women and Indian artist received commissions. Taken together the works exhibited by the Section in post offices all over the nation offer an impressive tribute to the New Deal and its effort to bring art to the masses.

Chapter V

The following chapter is reprinted from an article in the *Federal Times* of March 26, 1990 by Mark Kodama. Reprint Courtesy of *Federal Times*. Copyright by Times Journal Company. Springfield, Virginia.

Remembering '70: Workers Risk It All in Historic Strike

Twenty years ago Bill Bradley, Cazzie Russell and Walt Frazier were leading the New York Knicks to their first division championship in years. Kareem Abdul-Jabbar, then Lew Alcindor, was enjoying a fine rookie season with the Milwaukee Bucks. "Patton" and "Hello Dolly" were hits in the movie theatres.

The Professional Air Traffic Controllers Organization was threatening to strike over wages and working conditions.

Twenty years ago on St. Patrick's Day, the country was embroiled in the Vietnam War. On that day, Branch 36 of the National Association of Letter Carriers voted to go on strike, touching off the largest wildcat strike in U.S. history and the only nationwide strike in postal history.

The strikers defied federal law, President Richard Nixon, Congress, federal judges, the Post Office Department and other national leaders. The strikers stayed out even under the threat of fines, jail sentences and losing their jobs.

"It changed everything," said Thomas Germano, one of the strikers and now director of the Cornell University industrial relations department in Old Westbury, N.Y. Germano, who later became executive vice president of Local 36 is writing a book about the strike. "More changed in eight days than in 200 years prior to that-certainly more rapid and lasting changes."

According to accounts from *The New York Times, New York Post, Federal Times, Washington Star* and interviews with postal workers who participated in the strike, this is how events unfolded.

A pay bill was languishing before Congress. The House and Senate had passed pay legislation the year before, but the versions had to be reconciled.

Nixon refused to approve a pay raise until Congress agreed to "postal reforms," making the postal service an independent government agency that would be run like a business.

"There was just an impossible feeling," said Jack Schecter, a retired letter carrier. Congress was supposed to have given postal workers a cost-of-living increase in the fall, he said.

Wages were so low that 7 percent of the full-time career postal workers in New York City qualified for welfare. And it took letter carriers 21 years to reach top pay. Carriers were moonlighting or their wives were working, Schecter said. "It was a joke, and it wasn't a joke. A lot of them drove a hack."

MARCH 17, 1970

Despite a threat by James Rademacher, President of the National Association of Letter Carriers, to suspend Branch 36 and any other local that goes on strike, letter carriers gather at the Manhattan Center on West 34th Street in New York City for a strike vote.

"There was no leadership," said Arthur Ullman, president of Branch 36, "People just did what they had to do."

Letter carriers in Branch 36 raise the victory sign and others shout, "Go! Go! Go! Militant members boo local President Gustave Johnson as he urges workers to stay on their jobs.

Then Johnson reads the results-1,555 for and 1,055 against.
The strike is on.

Moe Biller, President of the Manhattan and Bronx Postal
Union, also is booed by the crowd when he refuses to call a strike
vote. He does tell his members to honor the picket line, key to the
striker's success.

Later that night, the Brooklyn Branch 41 NALC local led by
Jack Leventhal votes to strike.

"The working conditions were bad," said former American
Postal Workers Union Research and Education Director, Michael
Zullo. "People had enough. It took the letter carriers to do it. They
did it and it started snowballing."

MARCH 18th

The first people to go on strike in New York City are routers,
the NALC members who sort mail for carriers. Picket lines begin
sprouting up shortly after midnight.

"At my station, I was the first one there," Ullman said. When
clerks came to work, Ullman asked them, "Will you honor our
picket line? They said they would walk with us."

By refusing to cross picket lines and joining the strikers, the
clerks shut down mail flow to Wall Street, law firms, department
stores, airlines and Social Security recipients. About 36,000 of
the 40,000 postal workers in the city are on strike. Millions of
pieces of mail back up at the Main Post Office.

National Association of Postal Supervisors President Rubin
Handelman, then a supervisor in New York City, recalls that
supervisors did not even try to sort the mail-it was hopeless. They
simply guarded the mail.

Postmaster General Winton Blount orders all post offices to
quit sending mail to New York City and declares strikers on a
non-pay status. He threatens to "determine the illegal activity
involved in the work stoppage."

The strike, once unleashed, takes on a life of its own. One local president resigns after his local votes to strike, other presidents are shouted down by an angry rank-and-file. Three thousand postal clerks of the Manhattan and Bronx Postal Union demand a sympathy strike at the Statler Hilton Hotel.

The New York Times reports; "Shouting 'Strike! Strike! Strike!' the union members swarmed over the speaker's platform and forced local president, Morris Biller, to flee through the kitchen."

"They refused to listen to his argument that union bylaws required a secret ballot in any strike vote. Mr. Biller said later that he hoped to be able to inform his membership of the date for a strike vote today," the paper said.

The strike spreads to New Jersey and Stamford, Conn.

Frank Orapello, now executive vice president of Branch 36, said he was feeling a mixture of exhilaration and fear. "I knew we broke the law, but I felt we were pushed into I felt we did the right thing. The public was with us."

MARCH 19th

The strike spreads to Philadelphia, Cincinnati, Pittsburgh, Boston, Houston, Akron, Ohio; Minneapolis-St. Paul, Buffalo, New York., Newark, New Jersey, and New Haven, Conn. Brooklyn United Federation of Postal Clerks President, Ben Zemsky, blow horn in hand, circles the New York City Main Post Office in a car, exhorting the strikers on. "By going around the block all the time we scared the scabs off," Zemsky said. Before the strike is over, about a quarter of a million workers walk off their jobs.

Chairmen of the Senate and House Post Office Committees, Sen. Gale McGee of Wyoming, and Rep. Thadeus J. Dulski of New York, said Congress was not going to be stampeded into approving a raise.

The New York Times, while saying postal workers had justified grievances, said the workers should return to their jobs.

NALC National President Rademacher summons 300 local presidents to Washington, D.C. to discuss a course of action.

MARCH 20

Labor Secretary George Shultz meets with the heads of seven major postal unions. The strike spreads to Chicago, Cleveland, Denver, Los Angeles and San Francisco.

"I am very confident I can sell this pact," Rademacher tells *The New York Times* after the meeting. "If I can, we are back in business."

The Pact: The Nixon Administration would negotiate immediately with unions if the workers return to their jobs.

Rademacher also agrees, however, to call a national strike if the postal unions and the administration don't come to terms within five days.

Shultz tells reporters that the striking workers may not be granted immunity for violating federal law. "We will meet those questions on an individual basis," Shultz said.

MARCH 21

Johnson brings Shultz's proposal to the membership at the Harlem Armory. According to *The New York Times* Johnson said, "A proposition has been offered, and in the end it is you who will decide. The administration has agreed to negotiate only after all the people have returned to work."

The carriers shout "No!"

"My brothers," Johnson responds, "These are not my words. This is what has been offered."

One carrier yells for a continuation of the strike.

"My brothers, your voice is loud and clear. And I will lead you."

The strike is reaching its peak. The Manhattan and Bronx Postal Union representing 26,000 clerks under Biller overwhelmingly vote to join the strike, Albany, Syracuse and Rochester, N.Y., and Providence, R.I. join.

A federal judge orders Johnson and other Branch 36 officers to appear in court on contempt charges. Nixon hints that he will use the National Guard to sort and deliver mail.

MARCH 23

President Nixon on national television urges workers to return to work. "What has occurred here is that some employees of the federal government are now not only going against the best interest and best traditions of their service, but against the recommendations of their national union leaders, against the oath of office that they took, against orders handed down by the federal courts, and they are cutting off service essential to thousands, millions of Americans," Nixon said.

"What is at issue then is the survival of government based upon law."

MARCH 24

The strike begins to falter in some parts of the country. Some strikers return to work in Buffalo, NewYork., Cincinnati, Trenton, New Jersey, Pittsburgh, Milwaukee, Bridgeport and New Haven, Conn.

Although the New York locals continue to strike, they become more and more isolated as troops sort the mail. Pressure builds to resolve the strike.

The Senate and House conferees agree to meet the next day to begin working on pay legislation. AFL-CIO President George Meany urges workers to return to their jobs.

Federal Judge Frederick van Pelt Bryan finds Branch 36 in contempt of court and orders it to pay $10,000 in fines if its members do not return to work the next day. Bryan orders the local to pay $20,000 the following day, $30,000 the next and $40,000 the next.

Johnson says he will go to jail, but Bryan says he does not want to make a martyr of him. Johnson, who earns $13,000 a year is ordered to pay $500 each day the local stays out.

MARCH 25

The leaders of the seven major postal unions, James Gilden, executive assistant to Meany and the postal service meet in Washington, D.C. National leaders agree to begin bargaining for a 12 percent pay raise and full payment of health care benefits, top pay after eight years, collective bargaining rights and amnesty for strikers.

Biller and Johnson call an end to the strike, and workers return to their jobs. Ullman and Germano contend that if the strike had held out longer they could have won more concessions. But many national leaders fear that a longer strike would have lost public support and the government would have moved to break the unions. Nevertheless the strike forever changed the postal service, unions and working conditions for postal workers.

AFTERMATH

In August 1970, Nixon signed the Postal Reorganization Act, the foundation of the modern postal service. Workers received a 14.46 percent pay increase, 6 percent retroactive to December 1969.

No longer called the Post Office Department, the postal service underwent a financial metamorphosis—it was required to break even. In 1970, 10 percent of postal revenues came from federal subsidies. Today, the postal service receives no subsidies and must break even based upon revenue.

The relationship with Congress also changed. Congress is still responsible for oversight, but it no longer sets pay. Unions bargain with management. Political patronage ended, and postmasters and supervisors instead were promoted based on competence. People used to "buy" supervisory jobs by buying large blocks of tickets from local ethnic and community clubs," Cornell's Germano said. "Politicians used to intercede on behalf of their postal worker constituents," he said.

The strike also brought changes to the unions. New younger leaders were voted into office and many of the old guard were swept away. The strike propelled letter carrier Vincent Sombrotto to the Branch 36 presidency and eventually to his present position as NALC president. Although Sombrotto stayed in the background during the strike, he was a driving force for change before the strike.

"For Sombrotto, it was everything," Germano said.

Biller also emerged as a winner. Biller's appearance at the picket line to encourage the workers to stand fast helped him capture his position as the national president of the American Postal Workers Union.

Pay and working conditions improved. Employees also were given a grievance procedure.

"It showed that the postal worker was not the docile person everybody thought he was," Germano said. "He was willing to put it all on the line to improve his working conditions."

Chapter VI

Stamp Collecting

The following chapter contains information excerpted from *STORIES BEHIND THE STAMPS* by Doug Storer. The Soliloquy of a Postage Stamp was also borrowed from that fine book. The Stamp History of the Baltic Nation was reprinted from an article that appeared in The Sunday *New York Times* of April 1st, 1990.

Soliloquy of a Postage Stamp

I am the world's greatest traveler. I've journeyed from pole to pole, and all the climes between...by dogsled, camel and horseback, by every land, sea and air conveyance, even by submarine, dirigible and rocket.

I am the world's greatest art and portrait gallery. The heroes and heroines of mythology pose within my borders. I portray the greats and near greats of all times; Kings and Queens, Pharaohs and presidents, princes and princesses, poets and patriots, emperors and explorers, athletes, architects, aviators, artist and adventurers, tribal chiefs, inventors, moguls, musicians and martyrs, dramatist and novelist, shahs, sultans, saints and sinners. Even the vanished forms of the phoenix, dragon, centaur and unicorn appear upon my face.

I am the world's greatest picture chronicle and miniature encyclopedia. I map communities, countries and continents, and reveal views from every strange remote corner of the earth. I

48

depict mountains and valleys, monuments, temples and ruins of temples: and every type of locomotion from automobiles to zeppelins and steamboats to space ships. I delineate all matter of sports, handicraft, customs, sacred rites and ceremonies; and nearly every variety of bird, animal, fish, fruit and flower.

I frame the horrors of war, the blessings of peace, the hardships of emigration, the plight of indigence and the blight of famine. I illustrate the adventures of Don Quixote, the fairytale of childhood and the legends of all civilizations. I reflect the symbols of art and culture, of natural resources and industry, of trade and commerce, of agriculture and architecture, and of all human endeavor. I commemorate the expeditions and voyages, and the inventions, discoveries and creations that make life worth living.

Millions of men, women and children are fascinated by me. Through my infinite variety they find boundless pleasure, relaxation and enchantment.

Yet... I am only a postage stamp!

One of our most avid stamp collectors had this to say about his hobby: "One of the best things about stamp collecting is that the enthusiasm which it arouses in youth increases as the years pass. It dispels boredom, enlarges our vision, broadens our knowledge, and in innumerable ways enriches our life. I also commend stamp collecting because I really believe it makes one a better citizen." This is how Franklin Delano Roosevelt felt about his hobby, stamp collecting.

Doug Storer in his book *STORIES BEHIND THE STAMPS* goes on to tell three stories about the fascinating world of stamp collecting.

The Twenty-Four Cent Air Mail Invert

A man named W.T. Robey walked into his local post office to buy a sheet of the just-issued 24 cent U.S. Air Mail stamps. He put down his $24.00 and received 100 stamps from the postal clerk.

As Mr. Robey turned from the window, he glanced down at the stamps in his hands. Then he stopped and looked at them again, all the pictures of the planes were upside down! As an amateur collector, Mr. Robey knew he had a great find, what philatelists call an "inverted center." Most of these errors never make it to the post office. They are found and destroyed by sharp-eyed government checkers before the stamps leave the printing plant.

To make certain it was a great find, he went back to the postal clerk and asked if other sheets showed the plane inverted. There were none. A check with other post offices showed Mr. Robey owned the only sheet like it in the world.

Mr. Robey sold these 100 "inverts" to Eugene Klein of Philadelphia in 1918. Mr. Klein paid him $15,000 for the $24.00 sheet. The sheet was later broken up and sold to collectors. The last price listed for one of the "24 cent Air Mail inverts" is a stunning $500,000.

The 2 cent Hawaiian Postage Stamp

In June of 1892 a well known stamp collector named Gaston Leroux was found murdered in his Paris apartment. The police were puzzled by the crime as Leroux had no enemies and nothing seemed to have been stolen. A sharp-eyed detective with an interest in philately noticed that a rare "Hawaiian Missionaries" stamp had disappeared from the dead man's famous collection.

Shortly afterward the missing stamp turned up in the collection of another Paris philatelist who had been a friend of Leroux. The man later confessed that he had killed his friend in a violent argument when Leroux had refused to sell the valuable stamp.

The group of rare stamps known as "Hawaiian Missionaries" takes its name from the fact that most of them were found on letters sent from Hawaii by missionaries who had gone to the Islands from the United States during the mid 1800's.

Postage stamps were first issued in Hawaii in 1851. Not many stamps were issued as there was only a limited demand for them as most Hawaiians of that period did not know how to write.

The value of the "Hawaiian Missionaries" is very high, and if you should find one in your attic, it could bring as much as $80,000.

The British Guiana

In 1873 a young English schoolboy was spending a rainy afternoon rummaging through some faded letters kept by his family in their attic. He was looking for some old stamps that might find a place in his album. He found a very dirty and crudely printed stamp but decided not to keep it, so he sold it to a young friend who also collected stamps. He couldn't know then, of course, that he had just sold what was to become the world's rarest, most valuable bit of old paper for $1.50.

It was the 1 cent black on magenta "British Guiana" stamp which had been issued in 1856 when that little South American country was a colony of the Crown.

The stamp was later sold to a dealer in Scotland, who thought it was a curiosity. He sold it to Count Ferrary, at that time the world's greatest stamp collector, for the sum of $750.00. The Count kept it in his collection for over 40 years, during which time it was established as being the only stamp of its kind in the entire world.

After Ferrary's death in 1917 the "British Guiana" was sold to a wealthy American, Arthur Hind, who paid $38,000 for the world famous rarity. When Hind died his executors were surprised to see no "British Guiana" in his collection. He had given it to his wife as a present and she wisely had put it in the vault of a New York bank. The "British Guiana" has changed hands only once since that time and today the old stamp which a boy sold to his friend for $1.50-is now valued over $1,000,000.

Stuck on Stamps
Carrier Calls Collecting a "Window on the World"

Anyone who handles thousands of letters a day is privy to viewing the great variety of stamps which momentarily pass his way. As a letter carrier I collect First Day Covers (new issues sent to collectors from areas of importance on the event being celebrated on the stamp). Letter carriers have many activities and hobbies they share with the general public. In the January 1990 issue of the *POSTAL RECORD*, an NALC publication, letter carrier John Lindstrom shares his enthusiasm for stamp collecting.

They're colorful works of art from all over the world. They're inexpensive and easy to store. And each one has a story to tell. No wonder collecting postage stamps is a popular hobby-one that delights children, fascinates adults and becomes an obsession for avid philatelists.

Many letter carriers get hooked on stamp collecting when they see the bright parade of postage that passes through their hands. But others come to the post office with a life-long passion for the diminutive treasures. One enthusiast is John Lindstrom of Minneapolis, Minnesota Branch 9. At age 59, he has been a letter carrier just four years but a stamp collector for more than 40.

"Stamps are a window on the world-a great way to learn about a wide range of topics and about geography, too," he said. A former high school history teacher, Lindstrom's specialty is stamps that illuminate U.S. history. He has collected stamps commemorating the year statehood was conferred on each of the 50 states, as well as issues showing when many became U.S. territories. At the 1986 Minnesota state fair he won a blue ribbon for his stamp exhibition depicting key events in Minnesota's history.

Stamp collecting takes its technical name-philately-from the Greek words philos, or "loving," and atelos, which means "free of tax." Stamps indicate that the envelope or parcel to which they are affixed travels through the mail tax free-that is, the postage fees have been paid. Stamp collectors are known as philatelists.

Though Lindstrom likes stamps for their educational value, he is quick to point out that people also collect them for their beauty, exotic origins or investment potential. "Collecting can pay dividends down the road," he said, "but you have to buy a lot of stamps to turn a profit."

Old and rare stamps in the best condition are the most valuable, as are some stamps with printing errors. Philatelists also make money by selling stamps to those with gaps in their collections. Because there are so many stamps, Lindstrom advises beginners to avoid the temptation to start an international collection. Instead, he suggest, "Start with American stamps and focus in on a topic." Automobiles, butterflies, the Statue of Liberty, Martin Luther King Jr. and sports are just a few categories he suggested.

Noting that the Postal Service will be an official Sponsor of the 1992 Winter and Summer Olympics to be held in Albertsville, France and Barcelona, Spain respectively, he gave as an example his own 12-page topical collection of all the Olympic stamps issued by USPS since 1932.

Domestic stamps fall into four main categories:

DEFINITIVE stamps ranging in value from one cent to $5.00 are found on most mail. Their subjects are traditionally former presidents and statesmen, other prominent persons and national shrines. Printed in unlimited quantities for specific postal rates, they are available from the Postal Service for several years.

COMMEMORATIVE postage stamps-Lindstrom's specialty-are printed to honor important people, events or subjects of national appeal and significance. They are generally larger and more colorful than definitives and are printed in limited quantities. They are usually available at post offices for two or three months, or from the Postal Service's Philatelic Sales Division for about a year.

SPECIAL stamps such as Christmas and Love stamps supplement regular issues.

AIRMAIL stamps are used on mail to be sent overseas. Lindstrom collects "plate blocks," perfect units of four or more stamps from one of the four corners of a sheet. Plate blocks carry printing codes and serial numbers in their margins. The value of these stamps is enhanced by the fact they represent such a small percentage of a total issue.

Some collectors specialize in collecting coil stamps issued in rolls, which have two straight edges and two with perforations. Others prefer stamps from booklets, which have one, two or three straight edges.

Philatelic products such as first-day covers can also be the focus of hobbyists. First-day covers are stamped envelopes sold the day a stamp is issued or for a limited time and bearing a cancellation with the words "First day of issue."

Getting Started

Lindstrom pointed out that starting a stamp collection can be as simple as clipping stamps from envelopes received in the mail and saving them in a shoe box. When a pile amasses, soak a handful at a time in warm water until the stamp floats away from the paper. Allow them to soak a few minutes longer to remove residual glue.

Carefully remove the stamps using small tongs or tweezers-oil from your hands can damage stamps-and lay them face down on paper towels to dry. Place a sheet of plain paper and a weight such as a book on top of them to prevent the edges from curling. When the stamps are dry, store them in clear glassine sleeves-these and other collectors' supplies are available from hobby shops and stamp dealers-or simply file them in envelopes until ready for mounting.

With more than 19 million stamp collectors in the United States, advice for beginners is available from many sources. The Postal Service annually publishes a catalog of all stamps printed to date: *The Postal Service Guide to U.S. Stamps*, 16th edition, is available at most post offices for $5.95. The volume has color photos and gives current prices for used and unused stamps in fine condition that have been hinged. A smaller *Introduction to Stamps Collecting*, 31 pages extracted from the larger book, is free at post offices and includes names and addresses for further information.

Additionally, USPS sends representatives to elementary schools to promote collecting through its Benjamin Franklin Clubs. Teachers serve as club advisors, and students who join receive periodic mailings on stamp issues. Two associations to which Lindstrom belongs send members periodicals with information on latest issues and exhibits, as well as ads from collectors seeking or selling particular stamps.

For more information, write to the American Philatelic Society, Box 8000, State College, PA 16803 or the American Topical Society, Box 630, Johnstown, PA 15907. Stamp Collectors who belong to unions can find fellowship in the Samuel Gompers Stamp Club, a nationwide club founded in 1980 for those especially interested in collecting labor-related philatelic items: P.O. Box 1233, Springfield, VA 22151 or call 202-637-5327.

A lot of people wonder how stamp ideas become a reality. How did that commemorative stamp set honoring the moon landing become one of your favorite collectibles? It's a multi-year process that was explained in the January 1990 issue of *THE POSTAL RECORD:*

Stuck on Stamps
Many Are Culled, but Few Are Chosen

The unveiling of the letter carrier stamp at NALC's Centennial Celebration in Milwaukee last August was the culmination of a multi-year process through which new stamp ideas must pass before the presses roll.

Considering that the Postal Service receives about 30,000 letters each year proposing new stamps-yet issues only about 25 commemoratives-it is no small wonder that the 25-cent stamp bearing three whimsical letter carriers and the slogan, "Letter Carriers: We Deliver!" has made it onto envelopes across America.

A resounding "no" has been the Postal Service's answer to other such diverse proposals as a devil stamp for Hell, Michigan; a pretzel stamp with beer flavored glue; an onion stamp with the scent under a scratch-and-sniff patch; and a stamp honoring actress Marilyn Monroe. Instant rejections go to proposals associated with commercial enterprises and for stamps honoring individuals dead less than 10 years, with the exception of U.S. presidents, who can be commemorated a year after their deaths.

Suggestions for new stamps pour into the Postal Service from individual citizens and from groups with lengthy petitions signed by public figures. In 1984 St. Paul, Minnesota Branch 28 retiree Robert Danneker proposed a stamp to honor Thomas A. Dooley, the American doctor who returned to Indochina after serving there with the Navy, to found hospitals for the poor and sick of Vietnam and Laos. Danneker claims well over 1,000 signatures on petitions and personal letters, and support from such notables as Sen. Edward Kennedy, Gov. Mario Cuomo and actor Gregory Peck. But Dooley's cause has yet to meet with success.

Ideas for new stamps are screened by a 15-member Citizen Stamp Advisory Committee, whose job it is to suggest new stamps to the postmaster general. The panel meets six times a year to consider proposals and their potential appeal to a national audience. Factors taken into account include design, taste and reproductive qualities. The committee's charter mandates that it give the best advice possible, ignoring the volume of mail that may support a particular subject. Once an idea is approved by the PMG, the committee selects an artist to design the stamp.

Stamps
By Barth Healey

Fast-Forward History in the Baltic Nations Gives New Significance to the Region's Older Issues.

In a year of stunning headlines capturing the tumult in Eastern Europe, the one three weeks ago in *The New York Times* was among the most arresting: *"Parliament in Lithuania, 124-0, Declares Nation Independent."*

That a small Soviet satellite, however illustrious its heritage, might thus snub Moscow is one of the many remarkable images as history runs on fast forward.

Lithuania and other Baltic states of Latvia and Estonia are listed in most catalogues as "inactive," dead countries as far as new stamps are concerned. But there is a great wealth of older material. Lithuania was once a kingdom that stretched south along the Urals to the Black Sea. In the late 14th century, it entered an alliance with the weaker Polish kingdom. But over the centuries Lithuania's political vigor waned as Poland's waxed.

By 1795, Lithuania had become a vassal of Russia, and remained so until World War I. After three years of occupation by German troops, Lithuania declared its independence and maintained its singular existence until Soviet troops forcibly annexed the country in July, 1940.

The history of Latvia and Estonia is similar: early domination by Poland, by German martial orders and by Sweden until control passed to Russia in the 18th century; declarations of independence after World War I, more than two decades of liberty: reversion to Soviet control early in World War II.

The Baltic nations' freedom between wars was real; indeed Moscow recognized their independence in 1920. Washington, at least nominally, still considers Lithuania, Latvia and Estonia independent.

Collecting stamps from the Baltic states offers several challenges: there are almost 1,000 issues, enriched by overprints during German and Russian occupations. There are plenty of counterfeits to test the forensic philatelist. And there is the sense that in studying the postal history of the past, it may be possible to glimpse the history of the future.

Chapter VII

One of the modern problems facing Americans with increasing severity is homelessness. Paul Collier 46, a letter carrier from the Syracuse Branch 134 faces the challenge of homelessness in a unique way. Recounted below is one man's answer to a modern prayer—"to feed the hungry."

"We walk by them on the street-the people letter carriers don't deliver to, because they have no address. Estimates of the homeless in the U.S. range from 300,000 to several million, but everyone agrees that the problem is growing."

Letter carrier Paul Collier has chosen to see these invisible people, and he says that not only are their numbers increasing, but the homeless have gotten younger. The following article appeared in the February 1990 issue of *THE POSTAL RECORD*, a National Association of Letter Carriers publication.

Homecooking for the Homeless

A home and a hot meal-most of us take these comforts for granted. But because letter carrier Paul Collier knows that many people have no home, he makes sure they receive a hot meal in the morning. Rather than sleep in on Sundays, holidays and days off, Collier, 46, rises well before dawn to drive to the Oxford Street Inn, a night shelter for homeless men in Syracuse, New York. Parked at the curb, he dons a once-white apron and heats up the grill inside his truck.

Almost immediately, men emerge from the shelter—a crowded refuge from the bitter cold winter where they have spent the night. Their faces relax as they anticipate the warm feeling in their stomachs from a hot, home-cooked breakfast. Collier's specialty is a fried-egg sandwich with sausage and cheese on a grilled English muffin—and the men really go for it.

The Syracuse Branch 134 member allows himself a shy smile. "They like the egg sandwich a lot," he comments. "Many people say they're much better than McDonald's." His hands fly as he cracks eggs onto the sizzling grill, turns row upon row of hash browns, pours steaming cups of coffee, tea, and cocoa, and passes out fresh muffins and fruit. Bending slightly in a truck that can't quite accommodate his height, for two hours Collier bobs between the hot grill and the cold, open window where hungry people wait with anticipation.

Although Syracuse, like most cities, has soup kitchens and other places where the homeless can get hot meals, Collier has observed that many poor people still go all day without eating.

"By delivering right to the shelter," he observes, "they at least start out the day with good food."

For five years Collier has parked his breakfast truck at the Oxford Street shelter, and in that time the number of sandwiches he serves has skyrocketed. "In the beginning I cooked for about 40 people. Now we're up to about 90-that's the capacity of the shelter—plus others who come by from the neighborhood," "There is a lot of beautiful people out there who happen to be down on their luck." To Collier, hunger is hunger; he turns no away. To accommodate the growing numbers, the bearded letter carrier recently purchased a used truck to replace the battered "69" he bought from a farmer for $1,000 and a lawn mower.

Like its predecessor, the tan "71" Chevy Step Van is called "Catholic Worker on Wheels" and sports pictures of Dorothy Day, founder of the Catholic Worker movement, and Eugene Debs and Big Bill Haywood, union leaders in the formative years of the American labor movement.

Not surprisingly, Collier has parked at many a picket line, offering coffee and donuts to striking Syracuse union members.

Last year he pulled up across from the Hotel Syracuse, and while he served picketers, Branch 134 treasurer Bruce Bailey and Trustee Don Murray unfurled a huge NALC banner in solidarity.

"He is truly a man of conviction," says Branch 134 President Jerry Segovis. "All he thinks about is other people and how he can make their lives a little easier. He demonstrates solidarity in the full sense of the word—that progress for one is progress for all."

The branch supports Collier's efforts with cash donations, and several letter carriers have volunteered to serve breakfast to the homeless.

"They love to go out in the truck," says Collier, who works out of the Fulton Post Office. "It makes people feel good, to do something that directly helps another individual."

Collier also receives contributions from friends, churches and other charities to defray expenses. Food alone cost $140 a week, and he pays for the truck from his own pocket. Until he ran short of money, Collier did double duty on Sundays, first serving breakfast at the shelter and then driving the grill truck to the homes of several needy families, where he would cook hot meals to order.

"Anything they liked—pancakes, omelette, French toast, you name it. Delivered with a newspaper, too," he remarks. "I'm looking for a regular source of funds so I can resume that."

His wife Carole heartily supports his mission, often accompanying him on breakfast runs. They met through the peace movement, and both are deeply committed to issues of social justice and human dignity. Last year they demonstrated in Washington D.C. against the lack of affordable housing, and he was arrested at Griffis Air Force Base in Rome, New York for protesting nuclear weapons.

To Collier, the benefits of social activism are well worth the sacrifices. He has formed rewarding friendships with many of the homeless men at the Oxford Street Inn, where he stays one night a week, "keeping order," since it opened 10 years ago.

"One of these men was the best man at our wedding," he says. "Charlie's living with us now. It's wonderful to have a guest and to have a house big enough to have room for a guest."

His involvement with the homeless goes back a dozen years, when he walked into a soup kitchen on Thanksgiving Day to drop off a turkey. They said, "We don't need your turkey-we need your body," recounts the three year letter carrier, who was then driving a truck for a potato chip company.

"I knew immediately that I belonged there," Collier said simply.

When Oxford Street shelter opened, he began delivering food donated by grocery stores along his potato chip route. There he observed first hand the hunger that haunts the homeless, and started taking men out for breakfast.

But a $15 tab one day got him thinking about how many more people could be fed if he bought the raw ingredients and made breakfast himself. That's when the homeless found a good friend at the curb, serving hot meals with a warm smile.

Seeing the Invisible People

"I used to see older men at the shelter. Now, there's a lot of young men, some out of work, some working but earning too little to afford rent," said Paul Collier.

Many families are also on the street, competing for limited space in a system that is not set up to accommodate children, or women and men together.

Why are so many Americans homeless? Many were renters with no savings, living from paycheck to paycheck; loss of income or unexpected expenses resulted in eviction. Cutbacks in public assistance and the scarcity of subsidized housing put some families on the street, too.

Roughly half are substance abusers whose use of alcohol or illegal drugs is a major obstacle in rehabilitating their lives. About one third of the homeless are emotionally ill adults who have been released from hospitals. Unable to provide for themselves, they often wind up in the street.

"If there were proper supports for disabled people in the community, they would not be in the streets," Collier emphasizes.

Rootless Children

Whether fleeing abusive spouses or simply unable to earn enough to cover expenses, women with children account for one-quarter of those in shelters. These homeless children often do not attend school—a situation which could cripple their opportunities for future success.

Collier blames the government's economic policies for sending more people into the streets. "There are fewer jobs available now for people with modest skills that pay enough to support a family," he says. "There used to be more industrial jobs, but so many companies have closed or moved their plants abroad. Now all that's available are hamburger jobs, day labor, temporary employment, janitorial or security jobs."

"Our priorities are misplaced," Collier continues. "The government should be looking for new solutions that will help its citizens forge a better future."

In 1986 two million adults worked full time but were poor—a 40% increase since 1978.

"Once you're homeless, it's even more difficult to rise economically. Things an employer expects, like clean clothes and personal hygiene, become harder to do. You have no address, no phone," Collier points out.

At the same time the number of poor families grows, there is less affordable housing. Rents continue to increase and public assistance has been cut.

"This means that poor families have to pay a large percentage of their limited income for rent," he says. According to a study by the Center on Budget and Policy Priorities, 45 percent of all poor renter households paid over 70 percent of their income for housing.

Concludes Collier, "A family that has to spend that much for housing might have to forgo that expense and become homeless.

Chapter VIII

When a carrier has been on his route a number of years, he develops a special relationship with his patrons. The very young and the elderly, because they are homebound are of special concern to the carrier. The small child running up to the mail carrier to retrieve the mail for his mother and the grateful wave of an elderly patron signal a ritual that takes place millions of times a day across America.

Every carrier has experienced an act of kindness that deepens the bond over the years, an invitation for a cup of hot chocolate on a frigid day, an offer of a pair of warm, dry socks during frostbite weather or two aspirins that get you through an especially trying day.

The stories in this chapter testify to the alertness and concern that carriers across America exhibited while performing their daily rounds. They are a testament to that special relationship alluded to above. The first two articles that follow have been reprinted from the February 1990 issue of *THE POSTAL RECORD*, a publication of the National Association of Letter Carriers.

Watchful Carrier Saves Patron's Life

Cornelious Page pays attention to more than just his work while delivering mail in northwest Washington, D.C. The Branch 142 member has been keeping his eye in particular on one of his elderly customers, Roland Brill, who lives alone. Aware of his vulnerability, Brill had asked Page to watch for accumulating newspapers.

As severe cold weather gripped much of the eastern seaboard, Page had noticed that Brill's newspapers were beginning to accumulate. He knocked on the door but received no response. He promptly let a neighbor know, and she in turn contacted his nephew, who called the fire department. When the fire fighters arrived, they forced entry into Brill's home and found him lying helpless on the floor. Brill was suffering from hypothermia, as the gas supply to his home had been disconnected.

Brill was taken to the hospital, where he recovered. Doctors believed, however, that if one more day had passed before he was rescued, Brill would not have survived.

Older Man Gets in Over His Head

An elderly man apparently had fallen into an open construction pit along Herbert L. Coleman's Asbury Park, New Jersey route. As he struggled to extricate himself, he succeeded only in bring more sand down to bury himself deeper.

Seeing the top of the man's head bobbing up and down barely above the opening, the Branch 117 member raced to his aid. Calling for help to some construction workers who were eating lunch nearby, Coleman jumped into the sand-and-water-filled hole with the man and together they were able to free him. For his part in the rescue, Coleman received from the Postal Service a Special Achievement Award.

The following articles appeared in the January 1990 issue of *The POSTAL RECORD,* a publication of The National Association of Letter Carriers.

Bringing Relief to Quake Relief Workers

When San Francisco's killer earthquake hit on October 17, Greater East Bay Branch 1111 member Ron Bailey wanted to do something constructive to help. Remembering his days as a firefighter, he thought about the relief workers, police officers and firefighters trying to secure property and keep peace and order after the quakes devastation.

So the Dixon, California carrier, who works at the Travis Air Force Base post office, mounted a one-man campaign to bring food and water to those selfless public servants. Bailey solicited local fast-food restaurants and food stores for his supplies.

Armed with hamburgers, tacos and various other foods, he filled his pick-up truck with donated gasoline and made the rounds of the hard-hit Marina District, offering his cache to hungry and tired relief workers.

The response was overwhelming. Everywhere Bailey went he was welcomed and heartily thanked.

"You can't help everybody," the carrier said that night. "But you can help a few. If I wasn't doing this, that would mean that food wouldn't be getting to those hungry people."

Postal Walk Benefits Abused Children

South Florida Branch 1071 members recently participated in the third annual five-kilometer Barefoot Mailman Walk for "Kids In Distress" of Broward County. The non-profit facility is the only one of its kind in the Pompano Beach Area catering to abused children. Recently more than 300 participants, most of them postal employees from surrounding communities, walked the beachfront and collected over $2,000 for the program.

South Florida Branch 1071 member Ceil DiMegho spent four months during 1989 coordinating the event, which is named for the famed "barefoot mailmen" who from 1885 until 1893 delivered mail along Florida's coast from West Palm Beach to Miami, walking the beach without shoes.

Participants paused for a moment along the walk to gaze at a statue commemorating one of these legendary mailmen, James Edward Hamilton, who lost his life in 1886 while attempting to cross an inlet.

Among the walkers this year were South Florida Branch President Matthew Rose and fellow branch and organizing committee member Marcia Bell.

Open House a Grand Success

I worked in a small office in Nanuet, N.Y. Our Employee Involvement Committee consisting of Bob Casilli, Kathy Spring and Dave Yoffee along with Postmaster Aileen Wynne, Supervisor Paul Avila and Ass't Supervisor Bert Pages hosted an Open House for community residents. To our amazement 500 men, women and children showed up. The event was held on a Sunday. Ten carriers and clerks gave up their day off to host the event. Refreshments were served, souvenirs given out while designated Carriers and Clerks explained the inner workings of the postal system to the public.

Children wanted to see where their house was on a carrier case. Squeals of delight went up when the carrier pulled out a letter addressed to a child. A humorous and informative film on how a letter reaches its destination brought laughter and knowledge to the public. The film was shown eight times during the day to accommodate the crowd. A tour of the transportation facility and the sale of philatelic material made the Open House a grand success.

Two years ago the Nanuet Post Office raised $1,500 in a benefit softball game to aid the local fire department and ambulance corps.

OPEN HOUSE AT THE NANUET POST OFFICE A GRAND SUCCESS
Shop Steward Steve Hopper explains to children and parents how mail is delivered to their homes.

Participants at the Open House, pictured left to right: Paul F. Avila, Supervisor of Mails, Aileen Wynne, Postmaster, Bert Pages, Ass't Supervisor, Kathy Spring, Carrier, Dave Yoffee, Carrier, Barbara Hopper, Clerk, Bob Casilli, Carrier, Raymond T. Murphy MSC Director/Postmaster, Pete Mucciello, Clerk, Karen Avila, Clerk, Eileen Hegerty, Clerk, Steve Hopper, Shop Steward, Chuck Corcoran, Ass't Shop Steward. Absent from picture, Ralph Cabo, Carrier and Tom Riley, Carrier

TOM RILEY

Timely First Aid Resuscitates Baby

This article appeared in the March 1990 issue of *THE POSTAL RECORD*, a publication of the National Association of Letter Carriers.

Just as he was getting ready to place the mail in her mailbox, one of Gary Clinger's patrons rushed through the door and handed him a baby. The hysterical woman said to him, "Do something for it-the baby's not breathing!"

Clinger quickly turned the baby over and slapped it on the back, but this had no effect. Next he cleared the baby's throat and administered the Heimlich maneuver, likewise to no avail.

Noticing that the infant was congested, he decided to try mouth-to-mouth resuscitation. As Clinger blew into the child's mouth, its lungs expanded and the congestion was discharged. Clearing it away, he resumed his resuscitation, and soon the baby was breathing on its own.

While waiting for help to arrive, Clinger monitored the infant to make sure it continued breathing. An ambulance arrived shortly, whisking mother and child off to the emergency room. Clinger was happy he was able to offer such crucial assistance to his patron, but he doesn't consider himself a hero for it. "I didn't think about saving the baby," he said. "I was just glad to see it breathing."

For his life-saving acts, the Portsmouth, Ohio Branch 184 member received from his postmaster special congratulations, a plaque and a $500 award.

Human Chain Pulls Boy from Icy Lake

This article also appeared in *THE POSTAL RECORD* of March 1990. *THE POSTAL RECORD* is a publication of the National Association of Letter Carriers.

The frozen lakes winter brings with it are a boon to skaters and hockey players, albeit a dangerous one. A Wisconsin boy found this out the hard way—he skated over a patch of thin ice and broke through.

Luckily for him, however, letter carrier George Girard was passing by as he was beginning his route. Seeing Ben Ryder go through, he ran to the lake's edge and started out to him.

Sensing that the ice was too thin to support his weight, however, Girard instructed the 15-year-old to hang onto the edge of the ice while he went for help. The Menomonie Branch 1033 member enlisted the aid of three passers-by; they edged out on their stomachs, forming a human chain to reach the boy and pull him from the frigid waters.

Because of the swiftness of the rescue, Ryder did not require medical attention.

The following three articles appeared in the March 1990 issue of *THE POSTAL RECORD.*

Tampa Carriers Aid Hurricane Victims

After Hurricane Hugo ripped across South Carolina last fall, leaving in its wake a path of destruction miles wide, an outpouring of relief supplies began flooding into the devastated areas. Because of extensive disruptions in the transportation system, however, it became difficult to distribute supplies to the hurricane victims.

You can imagine then the surprise of the residents of McClellanville, St. Stephens, Cross, and Moncks Corner when their letter carriers arrived bearing Christmas gifts.

"I realized they weren't going to have much of a Christmas without help," said Tampa, Florida Branch 599 member Bob McCarthy, so he organized a system of collecting and distributing Christmas gifts to hurricane victims.

Robert O' Neill, postmaster of Brandon, Florida and McCarthy's boss, was enthusiastic about the idea, too. He phoned his friend, postmaster of Charleston, to coordinate the effort, McCarthy and other Tampa letter carriers solicited donations of new clothing, toys and other useful items, wrapped and ready for giving, from their patrons. These gifts were sent to South Carolina for distribution by letter carriers there to those most in need.

"Who knows better than the carriers which families are the neediest? I thought it would be wonderful if we could use that army of knowledge to make things better," he said.

Mace in Face Deters More Than Dogs

While waiting in her car to pick up her granddaughter from school one afternoon, a Miami woman was approached by two women on foot, one of whom was wielding a knife. The woman with the knife opened the car door and began pulling the driver from it, despite her screams of protest.

Aware of the assault, another woman came running to her aid, but was cut by the woman with the knife. By this time, the driver had been pulled from her car and the second assailant was trying to start it.

Ron Snapp had also come to pick up his children from school and saw what was going on. He ran over to the struggle and sprayed mace into the faces of the assailants, who immediately fled.

The SouthFlorida Branch 1071 steward then administered first aid to the injured woman, staying with her until paramedics arrived.

TOM RILEY

Carrier Averts Electrical Shocks

Just before Thanksgiving last year, upstate New York was hit with deadly tornadoes. In the course of the storm, the LLV that Mike Schmitt was driving was blown from the road and landed against a tree.

The storm had also blown down power lines, one of which was lying in a puddle near another car that had pulled off the road not far from Schmitt. Inside the car were two elderly women, apparently quite shaken by the tempest.

As the driver began to get out and step into the electrically charged puddle, Schmitt ran to her car and kicked the door shut; in the process, he received a slight shock himself. He then explained to them the danger of the situation they were in.

The Glen Falls, New York Branch 81 member was able to right his LLV. He drove his vehicle to the end of the street, where he parked it so as to block the street's access.

Not only did Schmitt potentially save the lives of the women in the car, but he also helped avert harm to other drivers who unwittingly may have driven through the dangerous pool of water.

The articles you have read are true and just a small portion of the hundreds possibly thousands of incidents where letter carriers have been great assets to the general public during emergency situations. The author only regrets that the need for brevity prevents him from telling so many other stories and incidents where letter carriers have rose to the occasion when the situation demanded personal involvement.

78

Chapter IX

The U.S. Postal Inspection Service

Inspection Service Regional and Division Boundaries

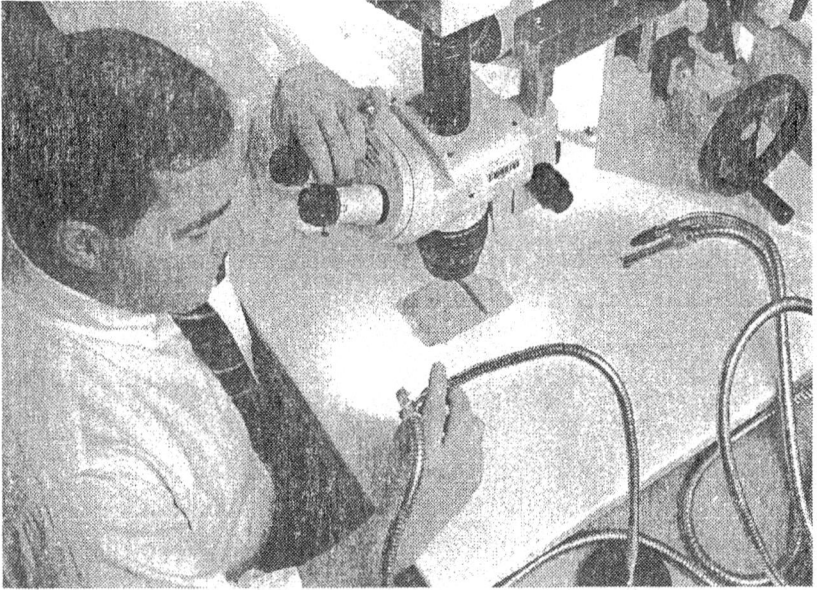

The Postal Inspection Service

While researching information for this book I came across so many helpful people who made my job easier by supplying me with great quantities of information on various aspects of the Postal Service. It made me proud to belong to an organization whose members were extremely knowledgeable, professional and so generous to the inquiries of an aspiring author. They not only gave of their time and materials, they also gave direction and new insights on where I could obtain more knowledge about our fascinating postal system. Paul M. Griffo, a Senior Information Specialist for the Postal Inspection Service shared the following information about our country's oldest federal law enforcement agency, The Postal Inspection Service.

The protection of the U.S. Mails and the mail system is the responsibility of the Postal Inspection Service. As the law enforcement and audit arm of the U.S. Postal Service, the Inspection Service is a highly specialized, professional organization performing investigative, law enforcement, security and audit functions essential to a stable and sound postal system.

As our country's oldest federal law enforcement agency, the Inspection Service has jurisdiction in all criminal matters infringing on the integrity and security of the mail, and the safety of all postal valuables, property and personnel.

Postal Inspectors

Postal Inspectors are the fact finding and investigative agents of the U.S. Postal Service. Today nearly two-thirds of their time is spent in investigating and solving postal related crimes. Possessing statutory power of arrest, they apprehend violators of the law and work closely with U.S. Attorneys in prosecuting cases in court. Their work also includes crime prevention, the audit of postal operations, investigation of accidents and a wide variety of other service and audit matters. They also have the responsibility to restore mail service following catastrophes such as floods, fire and train and airplane wrecks.

There are approximately 1,900 Postal inspectors stationed in the United States and Puerto Rico. All trainees undergo an eleven-week basic training course involving use of firearms, defensive tactics, legal matters, search and seizure, arrest techniques, court procedures, postal operations, audit functions, and a detailed study of the federal laws in which the Inspection Service has jurisdiction. Specialized courses are continually held to equip the Service with expertly trained personnel.

The upward trend in financial crimes in the Postal Service led to closer scrutiny of internal controls by postal inspectors. Prompt attention to the identification, removal and Prosecution of offenders was a high priority during Fiscal Year 1989.

A) Employee embezzlement cases resulted in 410 arrests, 386 convictions, and 837 employees removed from the USPS.
B) Abuse of workers' compensation benefits led to 39 arrest, 28 convictions, and 237 employee removals.
C) Crimes against the USPS such as counterfeit and contraband postage, money order offenses and vandalism yielded 1,001 arrests and 854 convictions.
D) Fraud against the USPS produced 50 arrest and 40 convictions.
E) Postal robbery investigations led to 84 arrest and 78 convictions.
F) Postal burglary cases resulted in 289 arrest and 253 convictions.

Protecting the Work Environment

The Inspection Service plays an essential role in providing a secure workplace for the 3/4 of a million men and women who deliver the nations mail. The reduction of assaults on employees, the elimination of drugs in the workplace, and the prevention of postal crimes are key factors in this program.

* Employee assault cases yielded 466 arrest and 343 convictions.

* Investigations of narcotics involvement by employees led to 451 arrest and 343 convictions.

* 3,615 presentations to employees and 918 facility risk surveys were conducted to improve postal security.

* Postal Police Officers rendered First Aid 638 times, responded to 1,422 assaults, answered 21,933 postal alarms, and escorted 30,840 high value shipments.

Criminal misuse of the mails range from thefts and mistreatment of mail, to the mailing of bombs and narcotics. Virtually every major fraud case prosecuted this year had the

TOM RILEY

Inspection Service insignia on it. Postal inspectors continued to lead the battle against pornography, particularly in cases involving children.
   *   Mailing explosives resulted in 98 arrests and 96 convictions.
   *   Mailing controlled substances caused 886 arrests and 449 convictions.
   *   Mailing pornography and obscenity resulted in 232 arrests and 250 convictions
   *   Mail fraud investigations resulted in 1,543 arrests and 1,225 convictions.
   *   Theft and mail mistreatment by employees resulted in 1,154 arrests, 1,107 convictions and 1,441 removals from the USPS.
   *   Mail theft by non-employees led to 4,725 arrests and 3,967 convictions.

Inspection Service Crime Laboratories.

A network of crime laboratories support field investigations with expert analysis of evidence and subsequent courtroom testimony. As they celebrate their 50th anniversary of service, the Inspection Service laboratories completed another year of outstanding accomplishments.
   *   7,272 requests for forensic examinations.
   *   3,121 postal offenders identified.
   *   221 court appearances.

Forfeiture

Forfeiture authority was expanded this fiscal year to include postal related drug and money laundering investigations. Successful prosecution of mail fraud charges in one Wall Street insider trading case led to the largest single forfeiture action in history, $222 million. $78 million was turned over to the Postal Service.

Program Fraud Civil Remedies Act

The Inspection Service was the first agency to recognize the potential for recouping losses which this new authority offers. Claims have been filed in cases involving fraud by both employees and outside contractors of the Postal Service.

Highlights: Among the many accomplishments of the year, these are particularly noteworthy.

* A task force led by postal inspectors convicted televangelist Jim Bakker and his associates of fraud.

* Inspectors convicted a Denver letter carrier who failed to deliver 3 tons of mail.

* $8.9 million in revenue deficiencies were identified by inspectors during the fiscal year.

* $78 million was turned over to the Postal Service as part of the forfeiture action in the mail fraud conviction of Drexel Burnham Lambert, Inc.

* Investigations of workers' compensation claims led to cost avoidances of more than $30 million.

* $80 million in funds which could be better used were identified in contract audits of Electrocom Automation, Inc.

* Separate investigations of schemes to avoid payment of postage in New York and California resulted in restitution to the USPS of over $5.5 million.

* An audit of proposed pricing for the new USPS long-life vehicle resulted in $4 million in questioned costs identified.

Internal Audits

Postal Inspectors provide management with independent audits that protect the assets of the Postal Service, improve its financial management, and identify specific improvements for better customer service and more economical operations. They also assist in the resolution of customer complaints and investigate matters of Congressional interest.

Conviction Rate

The Inspection Service maintains a consistently high conviction rate each year of approximately 98% of cases brought to trial, a rate not exceeded by any other federal law enforcement agency.

The Postal Inspection Service issues a Semi-Annual Report detailing the activities involving the organization. In the last six months of 1989 the Inspection Service conducted over 11,000 investigations and audits. Each case represents the work of one or more postal inspectors engaged in the business of protecting America's postal system and its customers. Inspectors apprehended 5,826 violators of postal laws during the second half of Fiscal Year 1989.

In the same time period 862 audits were made available to postal managers, many of them documenting commendable efforts by postal managers to improve efficiency and meet delivery standards. These audits involved more than 354,000 work hours and they led to improved postal operations. They also set a standard for future activities.

The following cases highlight some of the day-to-day business of the Postal Inspection Service. Included are the many facets of the work of the law enforcement and audit arm of the Postal Service.

Postal Vehicle Attacks in Los Angeles

The 8,500 postal vehicles which service the Los Angeles area became the target of an increasing number of attacks in the mid 1980's. More than 200 break-in's were reported in 1987 and in 1988. Postal Inspectors recognized that vehicles had become a favorite source for treasury checks, particularly among illegal aliens who were flooding the L.A. area. A team of inspectors undertook the task of both apprehending those responsible and reducing the number of attacks. The efforts of the team have produced 78 arrests during the first three-quarters of FY 1989. There were 84 vehicle attacks in the first nine months of the fiscal year as compared to 211 for the same period in FY 1988 and 240 in FY 1987. The reduction is the result of aggressive enforcement activities and the installation of security modification kits in every jeep serving the target area.

Springfield, MO

A pair of local men were indicted May 30, 1989 after a series of parcels containing child pornography was delivered to them via a post office box. Upon executing federal search warrants at the residences of the defendants, inspectors seized 400 video cassettes and a quantity of audio and video recording equipment.

Monroe, OR

Four suspects indicted April 4, 1989 owned the Monroe First Federal Bank, which consisted of a post office box and a telephone number at an answering service. They created the fraudulent bank to distribute counterfeit $100 travelers' checks. Search warrants executed at the delivery office produced four parcels mailed from Canada containing $320,000 worth of bogus checks.

Pittsburgh, PA

The pitch to sell a water purifier by mail included the promise of prizes which, inspectors found, were not being awarded. A

Temporary Restraining Order (TRO) detaining mail to the company was issued May 5, 1989. In a Consent Agreement the company agreed to desist from such practices.

Bombs in the Mail

There are few crimes more terrifying and potentially destructive of life and property than the mailing of a bomb. Strong laws, strict enforcement, and the likelihood of severe punishment if caught have made this a relatively rare crime. During the first six months of FY 1989 45 arrests were made in connection with investigations of bomb devices placed in the mail and bomb threats directed at postal facilities.

Grants, NM

On October 24, 1988 a parcel containing a bomb which had been mailed at Las Vegas two days earlier killed two women and injured a small child. An extensive search of the crime scene was conducted by a task force including Inspection Service crime laboratory personnel. Working together, local police, ATF agents and Postal Inspectors identified and arrested a suspect who was indicted by a state grand jury on November 9, 1988. Additional federal charges are anticipated in the case.

Waterville, ME

The November 23, 1988 sentencing of a juvenile to 8 to 10 years in the Maine State Prison stems from an incident in which two collection boxes were destroyed by pipe bombs. Inspectors and detectives investigating the incident identified two suspects and related them to other crimes including arson, burglary and theft of firearms.

In an effort to track down perpetrators who used the U.S. postal system in the commission of crime, the Postal Inspection Service established the Forensic and Technical Service Division in January 1940. The following article, *INSPECTOR'S CRIME*

LABS MARK 50th ANNIVERSARY by Mark Kodama appeared in the March 5, 1990 edition of *THE FEDERAL TIMES.* Reprint courtesy of *FEDERAL TIMES.* Copyright by Times Journal Company, Springfield, Virginia.

Postal Criminologists Key to Solving Cases

In 1973, postal administrators in St Louis began receiving threatening letters from an anonymous writer. By 1985, a flood of 267 letters had been sent, alleging administrative secretaries were having sex with their bosses to get ahead and other improprieties.

Postal inspectors zeroed in on a stenographer for the management sectional center, but they were unable to prove that she was writing and sending the letters. She denied she was writing the letters and refused to take a lie detector test.

The letter writer stepped up the attacks, writing vicious and threatening letters to the mayor, a principal, teachers, a PTA president, judges, police and firefighters. One letter said, "I have an Uzi that will blast all of you away."

In frustration, the inspector investigating the case sent the letters to a Postal Inspection Service crime lab in Chicago, hoping to find some clue to solve the case. Crime Lab Document Analyst, Roger Ball sampled the letters and found footprints on them. Evidently the writer was using feet to handle the letters so there would be no incriminating fingerprints.

Postal Inspectors foot printed the stenographer and then matched 88 footprints and three toe prints to the letters. She was arrested in 1988 and later convicted for sending threatening letters.

The crime lab had been the key to unraveling the mystery which had baffled postal workers in St. Louis for 16 years. For the 51 people of the crime lab, it was just another case they helped solve.

The inspection service crime lab recently celebrated 50 years of service. Crime laboratory analysts flew to Washington, D.C., lab from all over the country to take part in the festivities. Some, however, missed the celebration because they were testifying in courtrooms in other parts of the country.

"Our people are dedicated to the country and willing to sacrifice personal aspects of their lives when the job calls them," said Carrie Morgan Parker, director of the crime laboratory. "They do it on a daily basis. The people in the lab do whatever they need to do to get the job done," she said.

A big part of the technicians' work is testifying in court as expert witnesses. In many cases testimony of witnesses is not enough to prove the guilt or innocence of a defendant.

"A lot of times, it is decided on that (physical) evidence," said Dwight Holbrook, a senior forensic chemist.

"It's something they can see," Bill Roane, director of the crime lab in Memphis, Tenn. "It really aids a jury in determining whether that person is guilty or not. That is very important to a jury. They need that evidence."

The crime lab, part of the Forensic and Technical Service Division, was created in January 1940 when four innovative Postal Inspection Service clerks—Harry Ashton, James V.P. Conway, Albert Somerford and George G. Swett-put their hobbies of handwriting analysis to use in investigating crimes.

Crime lab technicians once matched a fingerprint of a bombing suspect to a piece of paper, measuring only one quarter of a square inch. The paper apparently had come from a note inside the bomb mailed to a victim. The testimony of the lab technician was the key to convicting the defendant.

Crime lab technicians in Memphis once linked a suspect of a stamp counterfeiting case by matching a fingerprint he left on a waste sheet of paper used to absorb the ink of the wet sheets of counterfeit stamps.

Another technician found a fingerprint inside a rubber glove that led to the capture of a man who had broken into a post office and stolen funds. He left his gloves behind.

"We turned the glove inside out, and there was an image of a thumb in that glove, which we later identified to the suspect," Roane said.

Crime laboratory technicians are centered in Chicago, Memphis, New York City, San Bruno, California., and Washington, D.C.

Chapter X

EARTH: Handle with Care

Letter Carriers spend much of their time outdoors. While delivering the mail they are often impressed by the care and beauty of the landscape created by their patrons and concerned when the landscape is polluted or the natural environment is threatened. Their concern for the environment is best expressed by Tom Brown and Al Ainsworth of Branch 82, Portland Oregon. This article appeared in the April 1990 issue of *THE POSTAL RECORD*, a publication of The National Association of Letter Carriers.

Letter carriers and alternate shop stewards for Portland, Oregon Branch 82, Tom Brown and Al Ainsworth love to work outdoors. Partly because they enjoy their jobs so much, they share a deep concern about the way society is ruining its natural resources.

"Letter carriers have a basic interest in preserving the environment," Brown said. "We're outside all the time and we've got to breathe the air, whether it's bad or good."

Ainsworth, 48, has been involved in environmental causes for years. In 1982 he helped establish the North West Rafters Association, a 500-member boating group that provides information to Congress and the public on issues affecting rivers. He also serves on the boards of the Oregon Rivers Council and the Oregon Natural Resources Council.

"Letter carriers, like all citizens should be concerned about environmental issues, said the 13-year veteran carrier. "The more we consume, the more we use, the less there is to offer our children and grandchildren."

Brown, a letter carrier for 17 years also belongs to several environmental groups, including the National Audubon Society, the Nature Conservancy and the National and International Wildlife Federations.

"The central issue of the 21st Century will be the environment," stressed the 49-year-old carrier. "It's been building for years. People are realizing it's not just a concern of hippies and the radical left. It's everybody's concern."

For both Ainsworth and Brown, environmental activism is like charity: It begins at home. "It's really important that people take control of their own lives—recycling their trash, using their cars a little less, cutting down the amount of water they use," Brown said.

"It's amazing how much difference individuals can make. But it takes some effort. You have to bundle your newspapers, recycle your automobile oil, and so forth. I recycle just about everything."

Ainsworth echoed this sentiment. "Why leave water running when you brush your teeth? That's unnecessary waste," he said. "People need to make that first step toward conservation in their homes and workplaces. Then we need to reach out in our communities, our states and nationally.

"It's our responsibility-we owe it to the future to clean up the environment and preserve our precious resources," said Brown. "I want young people to inherit a world that's relatively clean and good to live in."

Clearing the Air

Perhaps there is nothing we take for granted so much as the air we breathe. But chemicals in the air pose grave threats to human health. Working outdoors, letter carriers face particular risks from short-and long term exposure to thousands of air-borne toxins.

Anything people burn—fossil fuels in factories or cars, garbage in huge incinerators, even leaves in your backyard or wood in your fireplace-pollutes the air. For example, power plants that burn coal produce sulfur dioxide. When inhaled, it forms sulfuric acid in the lungs. Slow-moving cars spew carbon monoxide and other poisons.

"When we recycle, we not only conserve resources but also reduce the amount of incineration," noted environmentalist Al Ainsworth. "We just can't continue with our current habit of jumping into the car to buy something to then throw it away and have it burned."

Incineration is just one cause of air pollution. Auto and factory emissions combine in the presence of heat and sunlight to form ozone. Sometimes ozone is visible in the form of a murky haze. But visible or not, ground-level ozone can wreak considerable damage on your health. It constricts the body's air passages, reduces lung capacity and burns the eyes.

"It's bad to exercise in ozone-it damages the lungs." Portland Branch 82 member Tom Brown noted. "Letter carriers and other outdoor workers are at risk from ozone on warm afternoons, when the morning pollution has had a chance to cook."

Reducing ground-level ozone will take time, probably decades. Industries and utilities must control emissions and implement alternatives to current practices. But individuals must also contribute—primarily by driving their cars less and relying more on public transportation.

TOM RILEY

Troubled Water

Water may seem to be everywhere—in lakes, streams, rivers and underground reserves—but much of it is no longer fit to drink. The U.S. Environmental Protection Agency estimates that over 17,000 bodies of water are polluted. Contamination threatens the drinking water supplies for millions of Americans. In fact, some communities must rely entirely on bottled water, trucked in to replace the poisoned well water that residents have used for years.

Who is polluting the nations' water? Industries continue to pour waste into lakes and rivers, but some progress has been made in controlling this "point source" pollution. However, the greatest threat may come from the average homeowner and farmer. The many chemicals put on lawns and crops-and the organic waste they produce-add up to the very real problem of "non-point source" pollution.

Whenever it rains, water carries off pesticides from farms, fertilizers from lawns and oil from parking lots. The runoff eventually deposits these and other toxins into storm drains, water-ways and underground water reserves, known as aquifers.

Leaky Landfills

Water filtering through waste dumps also pollutes precious aquifers. A majority of landfills and industrial waste disposal sites, called surface impoundments, have no linings to prevent chemical leakage. Thirty percent lie in permeable soil on top of underground water reserves.

Such facilities are a major source of groundwater contamination. Water percolating through these sites, call leachate, may carry toxic chemicals into the soil and then into aquifers. Today, landfills and surface impoundments that handle hazardous waste must have liners and monitor groundwater. In addition, systems for collecting leachate are being installed.

Acid Rain

Along with point and non-point source pollution and groundwater contamination from waste dumps, acid rain-or more precisely, acid deposition—has contributed heavily to water pollution.

Acid deposition starts with sulfur dioxides and nitrogen oxides emitted by power plants, industrial smelters and vehicles. Once in the atmosphere, these two chemicals turn into sulfates and nitrates.

Washed from the atmosphere in the form of acid rain or acid snow, they ruin forest and lakes, killing fish and sensitive plants.

"Acid rain does more than destroy natural resources," observed letter carrier Al Ainsworth, a rafting enthusiast. "It ruins the recreational tourism-fishing, boating, and camping-on which many small communities depend."

Although the northeastern United States and Canada have suffered much of the visible damage caused by acid deposition, all parts of the country are affected.

Wasting Water

While America's water supplies are being contaminated by pollution, we are needlessly wasting what remains. The average American, for example, uses two to four times as much water as the average European. By conserving water-particularly in the bathroom, where over two-thirds of indoor household water use takes place, we can assure an adequate supply of fresh water for the future.

Hazardous Waste

Some of the material buried across the United States—such as carcinogenic chemicals and radioactive byproducts-is clearly hazardous to everyone's health. Such toxins are known to cause cancer, genetic damage, birth defects and neurological problems.

Over the past 15 years, federal and state governments have gradually tightened requirements for handling and disposing of hazardous waste. But American industry still generates massive amounts of toxic waste-about 2,400 pounds per person each year—and illegal dumping has not been fully eliminated.

There are over 1,200 sites on the U.S. government's Superfund list of top priorities for cleanup. And some government agencies estimate there are thousands more sites-perhaps tens of thousands—that eventually will have to be contained.

McDonald's Corporation and the Smithsonian Institution have published material on the seriousness of the disappearance of the rainforest. In a Future Globe report the following information was disseminated to the general public.

Lifesaving Cures Wiped Out...as Rainforests Disappear

Rainforest are becoming extinct at the rate of almost 100 a day and rising. We're losing things we take for granted and treasures that haven't yet been discovered. Scientists have thoroughly examined less than 1% of plant species in tropical forest for medical purposes. For example, given time, scientist may find a plant that could provide a cure for all cancers or other life-threatening diseases. The drug for childhood leukemia and Hodgkin's disease was originally discovered in the tropics, from the rosy periwinkle plant. In fact, one of every four prescription drugs sold in the U.S. today contains ingredients originally found in rainforest regions.

It is estimated that over 30 million species await discovery in rainforest. Rainforest are home to over half the world's plant and animal species. But an area almost the size of a football field is being destroyed every second. One-quarter of all species of life on Earth could vanish in the next 25 years. This means if deforestation continues, we'll lose thousands of things we already take for granted in our everyday lives along with opportunities for our future.

A better environment begins in our own backyard. It's not too late to work together to make a difference. Check your library for more information on the rainforest and other environmental issues. Be resourceful-get involved in your community's efforts to plant trees and recycle to help preserve the environment.

Chapter XI

Meet Former Postmaster General Anthony M. Frank

The following profile of former Postmaster General Anthony M. Frank was reprinted from the Spring 1988 issue of *POSTAL LIFE. POSTAL LIFE* is a magazine for postal employees and their families.

He drives the oldest Volkswagen bus in America, he admits he makes mistakes and wants his employees to know they can make them too, and he expects people who work for him to treat their co-workers as equals, no matter what their rank. Anthony M. Frank, former Postmaster General and former chairman and chief executive officer of First Nationwide Bank, had a reputation as an innovative leader who, before he started his new job, decided to find out about it from the ground up by delivering and sorting the mail.

Known as an astute businessman and an energetic administrator, Frank guided First Nationwide to 16 straight years of profits in an often uncertain industry. When he took over as chairman, First Nationwide was located only in Northern California and had assets of $400 million, when he left it had 370 offices in 14 states and assets of more than $18 billion.

He looks forward to serving as Postmaster General. "There are a lot of challenges," he says, "and there is also a great opportunity to serve the people of this country in partial repayment of the generosity shown to my parents and me when we came here from Nazi Germany in 1937."

Taking the helm of the nation's largest civilian employer during a time of change was welcomed by Frank. He sees change as not only inevitable, but also good for a company. "You cannot keep things as they are," he says. "You can either go forward or you can go backward. But you cannot stay the same."

Frank describes his management style as "monitored delegation." He says that means people who work for him get broad responsibilities and do their own managing. "But I need to know what they're doing," he adds. He thinks people are more satisfied if given responsibility to manage their own affairs. "And it's important for employees to be fulfilled by their jobs," he says. "I think we all work better that way. Shouldn't people look forward to coming to work each day?"

Frank is big on letting people make their own decisions, even if it means making mistakes. "If you allow people to take positions and then don't punish them if they don't work out," he says, "you develop an organization that lends itself to creative solutions."

How employees are treated is a major concern of the former Postmaster General's: "An overriding principle of our organization must be respect and courtesy for each individual postal employee, regardless of where they are in the organization. No one has a monopoly on good ideas. Everyone deserves fair treatment from his or her managers and co-workers."

He sees automation and work sharing as very important to the future of the Postal Service. "We are required to live within our means, and I see technology as an important way to bring down costs." In an interview with WRC-TV, an NBC affiliate in Washington, D.C, former Postmaster General said that "harnessing technology to keep cost in line" was his first priority. His second, he said was the "motivation of our people." According to him, "There is nothing more powerful than a motivated employee."

When asked if he would be constrained by the fact that as a government agency he couldn't cut the number of employees as many new CEO's have done, Frank answered: "I wouldn't do that if I could. I don't believe in it. You have to remember that your employees are human beings. If you can increase your volume and hold your work force steady, that's a very nice humane way to drive down cost. If you can harness technology and make reductions through normal retirement, that's a much better way to do it than go in there with some dramatic meat ax. Anyway, that's not my style."

Frank understands the importance of maintaining open lines of communication. A recent article in PSA magazine about how to handle the media held Frank up as an example of a leader with excellent public relations skills who had friendly ties with the media. In the article, Frank underscored his concern for treating other people with courtesy and fairness when he gave his tips for a successful relationship with the media: "Be available, whether you want to be or not, and at all times." His second tip: "Don't lie. Don't fudge. That doesn't mean you have to tell something confidential. Just say you can't comment on that. And," he added, "always remember to try and understand the other person's problems."

Some "Frank" facts about our Postmaster General: He is 57, 6' 2" tall, and he earned a bachelor's degree and an MBA from Dartmouth College in New Hampshire and did postgraduate work in finance at the University of Vienna in 1957. He likes to go hiking and canoeing. He is married to the former Gay Palmer, who was studying penguins in the Antartic when Frank accepted the PMG post, and they have a daughter, Tracy, and a son, Randall Palmer. He grew up in Hollywood, California, but has lived in Marin County with its reputation for "hot-tubs" and "laidback lifestyles, driving an old VW bus and serving on the financial advisory board of the Zen Center in San Francisco does not convey the image of a typical banker. But Frank thinks that all of this might be to his advantage. "People expect me to say and do unconventional things, so I can get away with more."

Not as colorfully, but perhaps more importantly, Frank served as vice chairman and later chairman of the California Housing Finance Agency (which provides financing for over 10,000 units of low income housing per year), and he also served on the boards of directors of four listed companies, an international company, and numerous local and national charities. Most recently he was a member of the National Housing Task Force, which produced proposed federal legislation this March.

Frank has enjoyed the visits he has made to the field and is impressed with the postal workers he has met. "I want to thank everyone for the surprising (only to me) pride and dedication to the Postal Service I have observed and for the great courtesy shown me and the willingness to educate me in my first months."

Don't be surprised if this unconventional Postmaster General shows up at your post office. "I like to get out of the office and mix with employees," he says. "I want to learn about the people who work here."

In the three years since Anthony Frank has been our Postmaster General he has brought with him a much needed era of stability. The previous three postmaster generals held the position for only a short time. He has been an effective administrator. The billion and a half dollar cuts mandated by Congress was achieved through cost-cutting and employee attrition, not lay-offs and firings. He is generally respected and admired for his attempts to communicate with his vast army of employees through his monthly Frank Talks, a newsletter mailed to every employee. In the newsletter, he lets you know what we're doing well and what we need to improve on. It's not all syrup and flowers and that's good because mail carriers can read the bottom line.

To get an idea how Postmaster General Anthony Frank can take the heat you had to watch "*ABC News, Nightline*" on March

16th, 1990. The Postal Service had just announced that stamps would go to 30 cents by February or March of 1990. Ted Koppel had Ralph Nader, the well known consumer advocate, James Miller, the former Budget Director, Moe Biller, the Head of the American Postal Workers Union and Anthony Frank in a live, televised debate:

Koppel: Let's start with the good news. Among the industrialized nations of the world, those, that is, that enjoy roughly the same standard of living as the United States, ours is the least expensive postal service of all, and that will continue to be true, according to the U.S. Postal Service, even after rates go up, as has been proposed, to 30 cents for a first-class letter a little less than a year from now.

Jeff Greenfield, an ABC News Correspondent, in a humorous voiceover went on to recite a litany of complaints in an interview with several actors who posed as members of the general public. They cited deteriorating service, delays, mis-sorted mail and inept personnel.

Greenfield: For some people and businesses who believe time is of essence, technology has provided a range of alternatives to the post office: fax machines, computers, satellite mail have all blossomed in the last decade, as have private companies who guarantee next-day delivery for 20 to 40 times the cost of a first-class stamp.

James Miller, the former Budget Director also challenged the legal monopoly that the Postal Service enjoys in delivering first-class mail. He suggested that privatization or increased competition from the private sector would make the postal service more responsive.

Moe Biller, American Postal Workers Union: "Well, firstly, I think Mr. Miller, of all people, has got a lot of gall talking about privatization, and he's represented the greed people in the corporate sector, and more than that, in his time as director of the budget, we—the United States has become, from the biggest creditor nation to the biggest debtor nation.

I think the founding fathers knew what they were doing, they set up a regulated monopoly for universal postal service at the same rates, regardless of who you are, you can mail a letter from Puerto Rico or Miami, Florida to Alaska and Hawaii for the same price. That could never be done in a competitive society. They would not only skim the cream off the top, but poor people surely would be unable to pay for mail service. And that's the great thing in this-the United States, that is, universal mail service at universal rates, and that's why a regulated monopoly is important."

Koppel: "All right. The postmaster general ought to have a choice here. We've had a lot of cracks taken at the Postal Service. You pick the ones you want to respond to."

Anthony Frank, Postmaster General: "Ted, I just don't know where to start. I'm the clean-up batter here, I guess after three people. We don't use taxes, we're the cheapest in the world, we do 40 percent of the world's mail. Eighty-two percent of the people interviewed by USA Today on the worst day of the year, namely, the day we raised rates, said they were satisfied. I think we have a lot to be proud of.

We are a business, and we're a public service. We do a lot of things that lose money. We do rural mail, we forward the mail, we have inspectors, we police against pornography. We do a lot of things well. We have to raise rates every once in a while. It'll cost the average family about $10.00 a year more, raising this rate by a nickel. I personally feel it shouldn't have gone up that much. It had to, but it shouldn't have. It should really have cost the average family about $6.00 a year."

Koppel: "I can send a fax and I can have it there in a minute or two. How much of an impact is that already having, how much of an impact is it going to have?"

Mr. Frank: "It's like measuring smoke. It's clearly having an impact in business-to-business communication, but in matters involving the household that hasn't done it yet, many fax—Ted, at the bottom, have my four favorite words: "hard copy to follow," Many faxes generate mail. Our mail is still doubling every 20 years, the volume of the mail doubling every 20 years."

Ralph Nader went on to complain about inefficient service, wasteful management and about how the cost of stamps exceeded the rate of inflation. While against privatization he saw a great need for improvement.

Koppel: "Let's talk about inflation—Mr Frank, what do you think? We've got 30 seconds."

Frank: "83 percent of our costs are people. And Moe Biller and his associates are very good negotiators and we did not, in 88, have the productivity we should. I'm pleased to say that in 1990 we do have the productivity. We're operating at one percent below the rate of inflation and I think it'll keep coming down. I really think we've got a handle on this thing."

Chapter XII

Privatization Exposed
Canada's Privatized Post Office Puts Profits Before Service

One of the issues facing the modern Postal Service in the future will be the call for privatization of various aspects of the Postal Service. There are those who advocate transferring government functions to private enterprise. They claim that a more responsive and efficient postal system would result if the Postal Service would contract out many of its functions to private enterprise. The following article appeared in the July 1990 issue of the *POSTAL RECORD*, a publication of the National Association of Letter Carriers. Those who advocate privatization should take a hard look at the turmoil it created in Canada's mail system.

When Canadians need postal services, they often can't turn to the local post office: it no longer exists. Instead, they must go to a "retail postal outlet" in the neighborhood food mart or gas station.

Canada Post, the government's mail delivery corporation, is midway through a five-year plan which includes replacing its entire network of urban and rural post offices with private outlets, contracting out parcel delivery and reducing such customer conveniences as street mailboxes and door-to-door delivery. When the restructuring of its mail system is completed, Canada Post will have eliminated 8,700 jobs.

The scheme to privatize Canada Post is motivated by the conservative ideology of Prime Minister Brian Mulroney—who wants to transfer government functions to private enterprise—as well as by economics. Mulroney is using Canada Post profits—revenue gained by cutting services and selling postal franchises—to ease his budget deficit.

The Mulroney government is pressuring Canada Post to achieve a 15 percent return on its investments by 1993, which the government would use to help balance its books and make Canada Post attractive enough to sell. The government wants to sell the entire mail system by offering shares to private investors—just as it privatized Air Canada in 1989.

But Canadian postal employees and consumers are fighting to keep this from happening. The 46,000-member Canadian Union of Postal Workers (CUPW), which represents letter carriers as well as mail service couriers, counter clerks, sorters, coders and maintenance workers, is spearheading the campaign to block privatization.

Americans who advocate breaking up the United States Postal Service should take a hard look at the turmoil in Canada's mail system. They would see that, far from bringing down prices and improving services, even the process of privatizing a country's postal system-let alone actually selling off the entire agency—produces precisely the opposite effects—and everyone suffers as a result.

Five-Year Plan

In November 1986 Canada Post announced a five-year "corporate plan" to close public post offices and restructure much of its service. The plan, which combines elements of outright privatization with steps designed to reduce service and postal employment, includes:

* Replacing all public post offices with privately owned "retail postal outlets" and franchises;

* Contracting out parts of the postal system, such as parcel delivery and vehicle and machinery maintenance;

108

* Trimming the postal workforce by transferring "surplus" employees to night work or offering them cash incentives to quit;
* Reducing the number of street letter boxes to cut collection time;
* Encouraging letter carriers to use their own vehicles rather than walk their routes, thereby increasing the number of delivery points and volume of mail each carrier handles;
* Substituting door-to-door delivery in new urban developments with huge cluster boxes called "super mailboxes";
* Eliminating Saturday postal service from virtually all public post offices.

Private Post Offices

Canada Post's most flagrant privatization scheme involves shutting down its entire network of 734 urban and 5,221 rural post offices by 1996, and replacing them with privately owned postal outlets. Already, many Canadians now mail parcels, buy stamps and claim registered and certified letters at makeshift postal counters inside the local video emporium or at the dry cleaner's. These "retail postal outlets" are staffed by the store's own employees, who know little of postal regulations and the sanctity of the mail.

Private shops first got into the postal business by selling stamps; but in 1986 Canada Post encouraged more stores to open postal counters and expanded their role to include parcel and registered/certified mail pick-up. Now postal customers have no choice but to go to these outlets to claim their parcels or registered/certified item, if the carrier cannot deliver.

Franchise Follies

In addition to these retail postal outlets, Canada Post is selling post-office franchises to the private sector—"much like selling a McDonald's franchise," said CUPW Research Director Geoff

Bickerton. In 1989, 153 such franchises were launched; 265 more are scheduled for this year.

Unlike the makeshift counters, the privately owned franchises are often stand-alone stores—the private-sector substitute for the public post office.

As both types of private outlets, open, public post offices close, eliminating thousands of career postal positions. Already, 200 of Canada's 3,500 counter clerks—called "wickets"—have received notices that they are "surplus to requirements." The union contract forbids Canada Post from laying them off; instead, surplus clerks are moved by seniority to mail processing plants, often for night work. Such moves sometimes prompt employees to quit, which cuts the workforce by attrition.

Post office closures hit female postal workers in small communities particularly hard, where postal employment remains one of their best opportunities to receive decent wages. Transforming post offices into private outlets has additional social consequences. When post offices in small communities shut their doors, residents lose their economic center and are forced to travel great distances for postal services.

Postal patrons have joined with CUPW in protesting the closures. Picketing in front of stores with postal outlets has been especially successful in strong union towns, where dozens of business owners have discontinued their franchises or decided not to open.

Contracting Out

Counter clerks aren't the only postal positions lost through privatization. Canada Post's five-year plan is eliminating thousands of mail service couriers, maintenance workers and other jobs through contracting out and similar machinations. Expedited parcel delivery, formerly done by union mail service couriers, is now being performed by contractors in nineteen cities who pick up, sort and deliver.

Shuttle runs between transport stations and mail facilities, post office equipment maintenance, vehicle repair taking longer than 30 minutes and security work are also being contracted out to the private sector. Management is also chipping away at the number of letter carrier and courier positions by centralizing mail redirection services and implementing new time values for certain job functions. Both issues are being fought at the bargaining table and through the grievance procedure.

The union successfully deflected Canada Post's plan to go to alternate-day delivery—a move which would have pruned letter carrier positions and, of course, substantially lowered the quality of service. At the same time that the mail corporation's service-employee payroll is being slashed, top management has ballooned by more than 1,000 in the last two years.

Have all these supervisors kept down the price of postage? Of course not. Postage has gone up an average of one cent a year since 1985, despite the five-year plan's promise to control rates. A first-class stamp now cost 47 cents Canadian (39 cents U.S.).

Canadians Favor Public Postal Service

Despite the loss of jobs and deterioration of service that have characterized privatization of Canadian postal service, Canada Post is charging ahead with its privatization plans. In doing so, it is ignoring the desires of Canadian consumers, and even the advice of its hand-picked experts, that service, not profits, is the responsibility of the nation's postal system.

Canadian consumers are making it clear that they want more postal service, not less. A recent national Vector Poll on postal service found that 77 percent of those surveyed favored extending door-to-door delivery to all urban households; only 19 percent opposed it. What's more, a majority of the public rejects privatization: By a 50-37 percent margin, they oppose transferring postal services to private businesses.

Even the Postal Services Review Committee (PSRC) established by the government in 1988, has had to remind postal-service management of its responsibilities to consumers. In a 1989 report, PSRC told Canada Post that its "primary obligation should be to provide adequate service to all Canadians." The committee went on to reject Canada Post's proposals to deregulate parcel delivery, money orders and special delivery.

Canada Post Corporation need not worry about opposition from PSRC any more: the government abolished the committee early this year.

The Price of Privatization

Privatization advocates speak in glowing terms of the supposed benefits consumers will reap when they have alternatives to the "mail monopoly." Consider the following events in Canada:

*   When the residents of Bloomfield Station, New Brunswick had their post office closed in 1987, they were given super mailboxes nine miles away. The rural route driver who services the boxes was issued a blowtorch by Canada Post to thaw frozen locks.

*   In Moorewood, Ontario, the private postal outlet has been in three different locations in one year since the post office closed.

*   In one part of Ottawa, Ontario, the parcel pick-up location has also changed three times since it was moved out of the post office. So much for consumer convenience.

*   In the town of Alylesbury, Saskatchewan, the post office was closed in 1986. The closest post office is now 12 miles away. You can buy stamps at the grain elevator, though, if you line up behind the grain trucks.

*   Across the country last December, the private sector's so-called "expedited delivery service" became overwhelmed by the volume of Christmas parcels, causing numerous late deliveries.

Union Busting

It's clear that management is pursuing privatization to break the back of the union. "Canada Post's contracting out is a cheap-labor strategy," said CUPW's Bickerton. "The church, anti-poverty and women's groups that support us recognize Canada Post's attempt to develop a cheap, non-union labor force."

Yet as much as CUPW's rank and file has been hurt by management's schemes, it is Canadian consumers who are paying the permanent price for privatization. For example, private post offices typically are little counters in the back of a retail store; postal service is a mere sideline. In contrast to public post offices, where employees average ten years of seniority, private outlets are plagued by high staff turnover. Security is often lax—parcels pile up on the floor and registered letters are within anyone's reach—and employees have little or no training in postal regulation. Moreover, most franchises are not accessible to disabled persons.

One privatization plan proved so disastrous that even the management of Canada Post had to reverse course. Until recently, Canada Post had contracted out "tier delivery"—the sorting and dispatching of parcels to small communities through central plants. But, because of numerous problems with loss of parcels and late delivery, the work is now being "contracted in." Canada Post has resumed doing work that private couriers were unable to handle efficiently.

Union Vigilance

The Canadian Union of Postal Workers has long maintained that Canada Post Corporation's services to customers need to be expanded, not cut back or contracted out. The union has argued that extending counter hours at public post offices, offering services such as packaging materials and stationary, and opening new Canada Post outlets would provide improved, more extensive services to the public—and employment for "surplus" workers.

The Canadian experience with privatization provides valuable lessons for the United States, said NALC President Vince Sombrotto.

"The turmoil in Canada's postal system illustrates how much all of us—consumers and postal employees alike—stand to lose from privatization," Sombrotto said. "On the other hand, the success of the Canadian Union of Postal Workers and their consumer allies in slowing down the pace of privatization serves as an inspiration to Americans who want to preserve the sanctity of the mail and a public post office which provides universal service at uniform rates."

Appendix

Postal Lore and Trivia

The following information on postal lore and trivia was supplied to me by Rita L. Moroney, Research Administrator/ Historian for the United States Postal Service.

DID YOU KNOW...

THAT the Post Office once owned a horse stable? In 1799, a lot of two acres opposite Havre de Grace, Maryland, was purchased for $220 as a site for a stable for the horses belonging to the Department.

THAT as late as 1872, a person convicted of robbing a mail carrier could be punished by death? The death penalty for stealing mail was first imposed by an Act of Congress of February 20th, 1792. That Act also included for the first time a fine for obstructing or retarding the passage of mail. In 1794, Congress amended this law to impose the death penalty only in cases where an individual had robbed a mail carrier. Penalties for stealing mail were reduced to fines not exceeding three hundred dollars or imprisonment, depending on the circumstances. In 1799, the penalty for the robbery of mail was changed to a public whipping or imprisonment of not exceeding ten years for first offenders. A second offense, however, was still punishable by death. In addition, the death penalty was imposed for anyone who wounded the person having custody of the mail or put the carrier's life in jeopardy by the use of dangerous weapons.

In 1810, the whipping penalty for first offenses was removed, although the offender was still subject to up to ten years in prison. These provisions continued in force until an Act of Congress of June 8, 1872, reduced penalties for second time offenders and the wounding or endangering of carriers by the use of weapons to a life of imprisonment at hard labor.

THAT The world's first telegraph office was maintained and operated as part of the postal service in the former Washington, D.C., City Post Office?

Samuel F.B. Morse, while assigned to the Post Office Department, opened the world's first public telegraph office on April 1, 1845, at the site of the former Post Office Department headquarters now known as the Tariff Building. The office was located on the second floor of one of two brick buildings used by the Washington, D.C., City Post Office, facing east on 7th street. The building was later torn down to enlarge the Department headquarters.

THAT The first telegraph message, "What hath God wrought?" was transmitted from the U.S. Capitol to Baltimore on May 24, 1844.

THAT In 1806, postal riders were given lanterns to enable them to travel at night?

Their instructions read "...the mail is not to stop except five minutes once in ten miles to breather the horse and twenty minutes for breakfast and supper, and thirty minutes for dinner."

THAT A postmaster delivered mail to soldiers on foot during the Revolutionary War because he lacked money to buy a horse. Ebenezer Hazard, postmaster of New York City and later a Postmaster General under the Continental Congress, wrote Congress in November 1776 that he was compelled to deliver mail to the Revolutionary troops on foot because he didn't have enough money to buy a horse.

THAT in 1827, one section of the New York City Post Office was reserved "exclusively for ladies?"

THAT The Post Office Department was one of the earliest consumer protection agencies of the federal government? Among the earliest legislative protection for the public is the mail fraud statue of 1872.

THAT The Postal Service once transported an entire bank through the mail by Parcel Post?

In 1916, in order to save transportation costs, a merchant named W.H. Coltharp sent a bank in small packages through the mails by Parcel Post from Salt Lake City to Vernal, Utah.

Although the transportation of the 80,000 bricks over the 427-mile route (there was at the time no road from Salt Lake City to Vernal) caused some problems for postal authorities, not a single brick was lost.

When Postmaster General Albert S. Burleson learned of this incident, however, postal regulations were rewritten to prohibit such large mailing. His letter announcing these revisions, which was sent to post offices, ended by stating that, "It is not the intent of the United States Postal Service that buildings should be shipped through the mail." Even today, customers occasionally send their belongings by mail in order to save moving costs.

THAT The Post Office once played a part in the weather forecasting business?

At the request of the War Department in 1872, the Department ordered postmasters in various cities be supplied with weather forecast by the Army Signal Corps, which were then posted in their offices for their patrons.

In addition, around the turn of the century, rural carriers delivered weather reports to thousands of farmers and rural residents in conjunction with the Agriculture Department. For a short time, a few post offices even experimented with back stamping envelopes with weather predictions.

The Postal Service also played a role in the transmission of weather forecasts during the period of early airmail flights. The Department began installing radio stations in air fields.

Beginning on August 20, 1920, and later, with the exception of Rawlings, Wyoming, all fields had stations on which plane movements depended on weather conditions obtained by radio. When airmail traffic permitted, other government departments used the radio for service messages instead of the telegraph. The Department of Agriculture transmitted weather forecast and stock market reports over them.

THAT Rural carriers once picked up groceries for customers along their routes?

Rural carriers have been known to take orders for various goods for the customers on their routes along with their other duties, including requests for such items as eggs, yeast cakes, tea, coffee, spices, and other foods. Carriers also purchased articles of clothing and collected and returned laundry.

In addition, in conjunction with the Agriculture Department, rural carriers have conducted pig and livestock surveys during this century. Carriers collected questionnaire cards filled out by a representative group of local farmers, who tallied their number of hogs and the amount of stock food raised on their farms available for hog feeding. These surveys were useful to farmers across the country in determining the prevailing market conditions.

THAT The Post Office Department has aided the Government in transferring gold worth several billions of dollars within the last one hundred years?

One of the earliest recorded gold shipments by the Postal Service was made in August 1892, when a special mail train loaded with $20 million in gold coin was transported from San Francisco to New York. The entire shipment, including the boxes in which the gold was packed, weighed over 80,000 pounds.

In 1914, according to an article in the New York Times, the Treasury Department also shipped roughly ten million dollars worth of gold coin from Philadelphia to New York City through the mails. The shipment was guarded by both federal officers and the police.

In 1934, the Post Office Department shipped a large quantity of gold from the U.S. Mint in San Francisco to the U.S. Mint in Denver. The mail was guarded by a detachment of regular Army soldiers.

The most prolific period of transfer of bullion, however, was brought about by the completion of the depository at Fort Knox, Kentucky, in 1937. In the latter year, over five and a half billion dollars worth of gold was transferred from New York and Philadelphia to this depository, involving 215 railway mail cars and 38 special trains.

From January 25, 1940, to January 23, 1941, shipments of bullion were sent from the New York Assay Office to Fort Knox. The gold, estimated at over nine billion dollars, weighed about 9,000 tons and was shipped in 337 carloads comprising 45 special trains. Its safety was insured by postal inspectors, Secret Service agents, police officials, and Army units. The Post Office Department received over $1,600,000 in postage, insurance, and surcharge fees for this transport of gold.

Between 1937 and 1941, some 550 railroad cars carried $15.5 billion in gold between New York and Fort Knox.

THAT Many postmasters once charged local patrons for postage on a monthly basis?

THAT The Postmaster General was not an official member of the President's Cabinet until 1829, when Andrew Jackson invited Postmaster General Walter T. Barry to serve in this capacity?

THAT Letters not picked up at post offices were at one time advertised in local newspapers by postmasters?

THAT From 1847 to 1857, adhesive postage stamps in the United States were not perforated.

THAT The Pony Express was not originally operated by the Post Office Department?

From April 1860 to July 1861, the Pony Express operated as a private enterprise. After July 1, 1861, it was operated under contract as a mail route until discontinued in October 1861 upon the completion of the transcontinental telegraph line.

THAT Russell, Majors, & Waddell, the company which inaugurated the Pony Express, lost an estimated half million dollars in the venture?

THAT The fastest delivery time for the Pony Express was in March 1861, when the inaugural address of President Lincoln was carried in seven days and 17 hours from the East Coast to California?

THAT The government issued postage currency from 1862 to 1876 because of a shortage of hard money occasioned by the Civil War?

As a result of a coin shortage caused by the suspension of special payments by banks during the Civil War, on July 17, 1862 Congress enacted legislation providing that after August 1, 1862, postage stamps were to be received in payment for government debt in amounts less than $5 dollars and were redeemable in demand notes (paper money). Subsequently, large quantities of postage stamps were bought in post offices, causing the Department considerable difficulty in its normal distribution of stamps.

Stamps, however, were found to be ill-adapted for circulation, leading to the issuance of postage currency beginning on August 21, 1862, bearing facsimiles of current stamps. This currency was issued in 5-, 10-, 25-, and 50-cent notes.

Postage currency was used until 1876, although the use of the postage stamp in the design of notes was eliminated by an Act of Congress of March 3, 1863.

THAT The money order system was developed primarily to provide a safe means for Union soldiers and their families to exchange money through the mails during the Civil War?

THAT Uniform postage rates regardless of distance were not effective in this country until July 1, 1863?

THAT Some postmasters made and used their own stamps, called "Postmasters Provisionals," several years before the introduction of adhesive postage stamps by the United States Government in 1947?

THAT Postage Stamps were used in a private City Dispatch Post inaugurated by Alexander M. Greig and Henry T. Thomas in New York City on February 1, 1842, five years before Congress authorized postage stamps?

THAT Over the years, postmasters in larger offices have, in effect, had cats on their payroll to protect the mail by keeping their offices free of mice and rodents, compensating the felines with food and shelter?

THAT The Post Office Department operated the telephone and telegraph systems of the United States from July 31, 1918, to July 31, 1919?

Under a proclamation of July 22, 1918, President Woodrow Wilson took control of all telephone and telegraph services within the jurisdiction of United States, including all equipment and supplies. According to the proclamation, the supervision, possession, control, and operation of these systems was to be exercised by Postmaster Albert S. Burleson. The telephone and telegraph systems, however, were returned to private owners by an order of Postmaster General Burleson dated July 11, 1919, effective on August 1, 1919.

THAT Benjamin Franklin, while serving as Deputy Postmaster General for the British, reversed his franking signature from "Free B. Franklin" to "B. Free Franklin?"

Although historians generally believed this signature was a commentary on the growing independence of the colonies from the Crown, it appeared on Franklin's correspondence as early as 1766.

THAT The postal Savings System, inaugurated by the Post Office Department in 1911, was at one time the largest single savings "bank" in the United States?

THAT Horse-drawn carriages were used to deliver mail in Philadelphia as late as January 31, 1955?

The 24 horse-drawn vehicles used along the narrow streets in Philadelphia in that year, rented from a private firm in the city, were replaced by a fleet of light trucks on February 1, 1955.

THAT The Pony Express charged $5.00 per letter?

Rates were later reduced to $2.00 per letter, later, under the Post Office Department, mail was carried for only $1.00 per letter.

THAT In 1813 when Postmaster General Gideon Granger was ending his long term, he had built up such a substantial mail profit that President Jefferson considered using it to help pay off the national debt?

The profit was $110,000!

THAT One of the most important byproducts of Rural Free Delivery was its stimulation to the development of the system of roads and highways in America?

In one county, for instance, farmers themselves paid $2600 to grade and gravel a road in order to qualify for rural delivery.

THAT A dog sled was used to carry mail in Alaska until 1963, when it was replaced by an airplane.

THAT Patronage was not effectively eliminated in the hiring and promotion of postmasters and rural carriers until the signing of the Postal Reorganization Act in August 1970?

THAT During the early 1900s, Postmaster General Frank Hitchcock ordered that all collection boxes be painted red, but the resulting confusion with fire boxes and equipment caused the order to be rescinded and the boxes painted olive green as before?

THAT The Post Office Department once received surplus motor vehicles from the War Department?

A provision for this transfer was enacted by Congress on July 2, 1918, and the Department began receiving these vehicles by November of that year.

THAT Postage Rates have been raised on three occasions to subsidize war efforts of the United States government?

Various. rate increases were in effect in 1815 and 1816 because of the War of 1812; from 1917 to 1919 as a result of World War I (plus a tax on parcel post packages from 1918 to 1922), and from 1944 to 1947 due to World War II.

THAT When the million-dollar Hope Diamond was donated to the United States by world-renowned jewel merchant Harry Winston. It was mailed from New York City to the Nation's Capital in an ordinary brown paper parcel?

The package was delivered on November 10, 1958, to the Smithsonian Institution in Washington, D.C. It was insured for a million dollars.

In addition, in 1979, the then largest uncut diamond in the world, called the Sedafu, weighing 620 carats and valued at $50,000, was sent by registered mail in this country.

In October 1987, an extremely rare red diamond worth several million dollars was sent to the Smithsonian Institution in an uninsured cardboard box. The postage for the package, sent by registered mail, was $11.58.

THAT Beginning in November 1983 the largest known direct mailing up until that time took place when some 70 million pieces were sent to business and residential telephone customers leasing Bell System equipment.

This mailing was the result of an agreement between American Telephone and Telegraph and the Federal Communications Commission, stipulating that AT&T explain the new telephone service costs under the court-ordered January 1 breakup of that corporation.

Postage costs for that mailing, which began on November 28, were estimated at $4.5 million and included letters to about 63 million households and seven million commercial addresses.

In May and June 1988, an even larger mailing was accomplished by the Postal Service, when a government brochure entitled "Understanding Aids" was distributed to just under 107 million households and post office boxes. It is believed to be the largest single mailing in history.

THAT The female head of a post office is always called a postmaster, never a postmistress?

THAT On July 20, 1969, Astronaut Neil A Armstrong cancelled the first piece of mail carried to the moon with a postmark which read "Moon Landing, U.S.A.?"

THAT Roswell Beardsley served as postmaster of North Lansing, New York, Post Office for over 74 years?

He was appointed on June 28, 1828, and served under 20 Presidents and 34 Postmasters General.

John N. VanZandt served as postmaster of the Blawenburg, New Jersey, Post Office for over 69 years. He was appointed April 23, 1866, and served until his death on July 16, 1935.

THAT David J. Travenner reached the age of 100 while serving as the postmaster of the Philomont, Virginia, Post Office?

He was 99 years old at the time of a press release dated May 23, 1923, and his successor was not appointed until January 5, 1925.

THAT The Hinsdale, New Hampshire, Post Office has been operating continuously in the same building since 1816, longer than any known post office in the United States?

THAT Lake Jackson, Texas, named two streets going in the opposite directions "This Way" and "That Way?"

Apparently, the townspeople liked the names as they now have other streets called Circle Way, Any Way, Parking Way, and Center Way.

THAT In 1961, Florida and Texas mothers irately returned hundreds of Patrick Henry stamps they had bought for wedding announcements, because the stamps bear the inscription "Give Me Liberty or Give me Death?"

THAT At Leola, Pennsylvania, when a new post office was being built in 1962, the postmaster requested a hitching post be installed because of heavy horse and wagon traffic?

P.S. It's still there.

THAT 2,781 letter carriers were bitten by dogs in Fiscal Year 1988?

These bites can cause death as well as serious injuries, and are never funny to either the Postal Service or the Carrier involved. Less serious animal attacks, however, have been recorded by one carrier who was bitten by a goose and another who landed in the hospital after being bitten by a bantam rooster. As usual, however, a Texan carrier probably holds the record for the "tallest" animal story, after claiming he was chased from a house five times by a "bunny" rabbit a child received for Easter.

THAT Not too long ago, a substitute mail carrier in Vermont received a box of baby chicks to deliver on his first day of work, and because the addressee was not at home when he tried to deliver this package, the carrier, mindful that the "mail must go through," took each of the twenty-four baby chicks out of the crate and stuffed them, one at.a time, through the envelope slot in the addressee's door?

THAT The Barefoot Mailman of Florida trudged barefoot on burning sands to deliver mail between Miami and Palm Beach from 1886 to 1890?

THAT The Jackass Mail Line was a pack-mule mail service between San Antonio and San Diego in 1857, and it was so dubbed because San Francisco and Los Angeles editors were unhappy that San Diego was the terminus of the first overland mail?

THAT A Camel Corps, using real camels, operated briefly in 1857 to carry army supplies and military mail between army posts and the tiny settlements of the American desert?

THAT In the mid-1800's, when postage stamps were introduced in the United States, they were often called labels?

THAT It was a mail courier who blazed the first trail between New York and Boston?

THAT It was a mail coach which brought into existence the old Boston-New York-Philadelphia-Baltimore turnpike, the first great American highway?

THAT The Post Office Department was responsible for the first night trains on railroads?

THAT In the early days, the use of the franking privilege to send letters free was more valuable to postmasters than the receipts from their offices?

THAT During one Christmas period, a temporary substitute driver, told by a postal supervisor at the Washington, D.C., Main Post Office to "take this truck to New York," meaning the New York Avenue Truck Terminal in Washington, D.C, mistakenly drove in the direction of New York City?

He proceeded to New York City over the Jersey Turnpike, and would have reached New York City had he not run out of gas and money for toll charges.

THAT The Post Office Department, in conjunction with the War and Navy Department, operated a service called "V-Mail" for the transmission of letters to and from servicemen overseas on microfilm during World War II?

The service was inaugurated on June 15, 1942, in order to reduce the weight and bulk of military mail and thereby create more space for vital military material, and to provide safer and faster dispatch and handling of mail for military personnel overseas.

V-Mail sheets were a combination letters and envelopes supplied on distinctive and uniform stationary, and were accorded preferential and expeditious sorting and transportation. They were microfilmed and later reproduced onto 4x5-inch photographs at various v-mail stations set up in both this country and overseas. Over a billion letters were sent and received from soldiers overseas from June 1942 to November 1, 1945, when the service was discontinued.

THAT In the 1880s, a dog named Dorsey was trained to carry mail unaccompanied on a route through the hills separating the mining towns of Calico and East Calico in San Bernardino County, California?

THAT Mail and supplies are hauled by mules eight miles down a winding trail into the Grand Canyon?

The route leads to the Supai Post Office in the Havasupai Indian Village, where members of the tribe still receive most of life's essentials by mail.

Chapter XIII

Automation

As we enter the 21st Century no other issue will affect the men and women who work for the U.S. Postal Service more than the issue of automation. It has been projected that automation will result in about 81,000 fewer jobs by 1995. The issue of automation seems to be inextricably connected to the contracting out of new jobs created by technology. We can't run away from technology by staying with the old methods of doing things. Technology is here to stay because it generates huge savings. We must prepare for technology by offering the workforce opportunities for training to adjust to the new technology. Leadership on both the management and craft side have to adopt flexible workforce rules that adjust to the new realities of automation.

An article in the *FEDERAL TIMES* by Mark Kodama:

Confidential Report Puts Job Losses at 81,000 by 1995 states many of the issues involved in the implementation of the new automated technology on the workforce. Reprint Courtesy of *FEDERAL TIMES.* Copyright by Times Journal Company Springfield, Virginia.

A confidential management report says use of automation will result in about 81,000 fewer jobs by 1995. Officials did not dispute the report but said it was dated, and they were revising the figures constantly.

About 141,000 clerk, carrier and supervisor jobs will not be needed because of massive deployment of new equipment, the USPS Office of Automation Integration said in a periodic report called the Corporate Automation Plan. That decline will be part offset by increases in level-4 clerk and Remote Bar Coding Systems positions if those RBCS jobs are kept in-house. A preliminary decision has been made to contract out the jobs.

In total, the postal service will be able to avoid hiring 102,000 to 120,000 employees by going forward with its automation plans, the report said. Because of modest volume growth, those figures translate into about 81,000 fewer full-time jobs in 1995 than 1990, according to the report. "The Corporate Automation Plan target decreases from 286,000 work years (in 1990) to requiring only 205,000 work years in FY "95," the report said.

There are 750,000 career employees now. The 286,000 work years mentioned in the report related to workers who would be directly affected by automation, Assistant Postmaster General Peter A. Jacobson for the engineering and technical support department told *FEDERAL TIMES.*

The report contradicts statements made by top officials including Postmaster General Anthony Frank and Deputy Postmaster Michael Coughlin, who have said the work force would remain the same size and that they did not have projections on how each craft would be affected by automation.

The report, dated January 1990 and presented to senior management officials, gives detailed projections on how automation will affect employees. Frank told *Federal Times* that officials have been straight forward about their automation plans, Frank insisted that the figures in the plan were estimates that were no longer accurate. "I think those figures are pretty old," he said. Frank insisted that the size of the work force would remain at 750,000 career employees because mail volume will increase substantially.

In the same July 30, 1990 issue of the *FEDERAL TIMES* Mark Kodama wrote an article that dealt with the issue of Contracting Out. The article was entitled, *Work Rules Force Contracting of 12,000 Jobs, Report Says:*

The 12,000 jobs created by technology that can sort hand-addressed letters have to be contracted out because work rules are too inflexible, according to a recent report. The new technology, Remote Bar Coding Systems, will require more part-time workers than the current 10 percent allowed in the national labor contract, according to the USPS report, "Comparative Analysis In-Service Versus Contracting Out of Video Encoding."

A tentative decision to contract out the job was recently announced, Postal officials stressed the decision was preliminary and that it could be reversed. The officials said they could save $4.3 billion by contracting out the work over a 10-year period. By 1992, the average contract worker would be paid $14.52 per hour, compared to $29.85 that would be paid to a USPS employee.

According to the report, more flexibility is needed before the jobs could be given to clerks for the following reasons:

*   Most of the jobs will require only part-time work. The peak hours for sorting mail will be between 5pm to 11pm and 2am to 6am. Workers will not be needed during slow periods of the late night and early morning tours.

*   The system for operating the equipment will change as more barcode sorters are deployed. When the equipment is first installed, operators will have to bar-code outgoing and incoming mail. But as other sites receive the equipment and encode their own outgoing mail, fewer operators will be needed.

*   Mail volume for the new equipment is based on an ambitious projection that 40 percent of the mail will be pre-bar-coded. Currently about 8 percent of the mail is pre-bar-coded by customers before the mail gets to the USPS.

RBCS equipment will enable letters that cannot be bar-coded on present equipment to be bar-coded and sorted on automation equipment. Deployment will begin next year. By 1995, there will be 295 readers in operation at 220 post offices and mail processing facilities. The equipment will be tested at two sites this year. The American Postal Workers Union has filed a grievance over the matter, contending that under the current contract the postal service must retrain clerks to operate the new equipment.

In the *NORTHEAST REGIONAL BULLETIN* of August 31st 1990 Postmaster General Anthony M. Frank stated the case for automation. "Our goal is to improve the value of service by achieving the lowest combined customer and Postal Service cost of preparing and sorting mail…To achieve this goal, we plan to have a bar code on all letter mail and non-carrier route presort flat mail by the end of 1995…"

The drive to automate the processing of virtually all letter mail by 1995 is fueled by the growth of mail volume, the need to make accurate and timely deliveries as America's population grows and the Postal Service's commitment to keep postage rate increases at or below the rate of inflation. Letter carriers could spend as little as two hours per day in the office and six on the street as the result of the installation of delivery bar code sorters in 1991.

Massachusetts Mutual, an insurance company located in Springfield, Mass took advantage of the new rates that gave incentives toward automated mail. They installed two Scan Code Bar Code Systems and a Bell and Howell Jet Star 800 Presort Machine. Now most of the mail that leaves Mass Mutual is pre-bar-coded and pre-sorted. The company has had a net savings year-to-date of $296,000 because of its newly automated mail operations. Before Mass Mutual implemented its automated mail operations the company sent the mail to a presort house, which sorted the mail basically the same way. In turn, a 4 cent discount was shared between Mass Mutual and the presort house.

Now, by sorting the mail in-house and using a nine-digit zip code they are getting a 4.5 cent discount on every piece of mail sent out. "We're obtaining the full discount where we were sharing it before. That's where the savings comes from," said a spokesman for Mass Mutual. Large companies who have volume mailings will soon seek to take advantage of the discounts the Postal Service offers to pre-sorted and pre-bar-coded mail. Many companies are purchasing in-house automated mail operations to avail themselves of the huge savings due to discounts offered by the Postal Service for such mail.

In addition to the cost savings, the new system is saving up to two days in delivery time to customers. In the past, the mail would have the next day's date on it. "We were losing a whole day in the presort process," says Watson. Often automation is associated with the elimination of jobs, but at Mass Mutual, the opposite was true. As a result of the new system, six people (two full-time, four part-time) were actually added to the staff.

The Future

Now Mass Mutual is looking at the possibility of "insourcing"—that is, working as a presort house for other companies who would drop their mail at the company for presorting, and share in the savings. Watson is confident that Mass Mutual's system could handle the extra volume, as he estimates the system could process 250,000 pieces in a 20-hour time frame, "We could probably handle 100,000 pieces in one shift."

Because of the advantages, Watson recommends using this system to other companies but warns that a thorough analysis must be done first. "I think one of the things that take a lot of time and analysis is looking at operations as they exist today. It took a full year. The teamwork between the vendors, the Postal Service and Mass Mutual was the key to the success of this automated operation of mail processing."

William R. Cummings, the Regional Postmaster General of the Northeast Region stated the case for automation in a letter to all postal employees that appeared in *THE NORTHEAST REGIONAL BULLETIN*.

"As the Postal Service heads into the 90s, all employees need to understand automation. Automation will continue to change the way we do business. If you are a letter carrier, it may mean that when your mail arrives at the station, most of it will be sequenced in the order you deliver it. If you are a mail processing supervisor, you may see that the flow of mail through the system is different than it used to be as automation takes on a greater role in the Postal Service."

The introduction of automation will enable the U.S. Postal Service to remain the best in the world. To retreat from automation and stay with outmoded methods would make us second rate as advancing technology would be introduced elsewhere to the detriment of the Postal Service. As the deliverer of 40% of the world's mail the Postal Service intends to keep up with technology as it has throughout its fascinating history. The letter carrier on the street will make sure that technology and automation which is rapidly being introduced will maintain its human face.

The Long Life Vehicle represents a significant advance in U.S. Postal Service delivery vehicles. Made with a corrosion resistant aluminum body, the vehicle is designed to last 24 years, three times the planned life of the familiar Jeep it replaces. The new van can carry 1,000 pounds of cargo, twice as much as the Jeep. It also gets more than 21 miles per gallon of gasoline. Because of its life expectancy and fuel economy, the Long Life Vehicle will save the Postal Service an estimated $5.9 billion. About 99,000 of the vans will be built by the Grumman Corporation under the largest single vehicle contract in the Postal Service's history.

U.S. Postal Service, Communications Department, Washington, DC 2O260-3111, (202) 268-2187 Photograph Number 87136-2-13, Credit Photo: U.S. Postal Service.

Chapter XIV

Understanding Your Post Office

This chapter is an attempt at improving relations between your local post office and you. This is done through better communication and understanding. When you complete reading this chapter, you will have a better understanding how your post office operates to serve you. I am always amazed at the number of people who do not take advantage of many of the services the post office offers. Vacation holds, stamps by mail, presort discounts on bulk mailings, temporary forwarding and Express Mail contracts are just a few of the services your local post office offers.

I've decided to enumerate some of the questions I am asked by my patrons as I deliver my route.

Question # 1—Is there a way to eliminate the unwanted or excessive junk mail I receive?

Answer—Yes, contact the Mail Preference Service. It was developed by the Direct Marketing Association to assist customers who do not want advertising mail. The D.M.A. updates its list quarterly, and once a person request this service, it may take several months before any results are noticed. Although it may reduce the amount of bulk business mail received, the service cannot eliminate it totally. (Information about the D.M.A. was supplied by Ellen Newell Call, Postmaster of Boothbay Harbor, Me. in the October 15th issue of *TIME* magazine)

Question # 2—I have bees making a nest in my mailbox, what can I do to keep them away?

Answer—In the spring and summer bees and other insects find mailboxes to be the perfect haven for nesting. Every year patrons and carriers are reported stung by flying insects, occasionally serious medical problems ensue. If you place a mothball at the back of your mailbox, it will be insect-free. (Answer supplied by Chuck Corcoran, fellow carrier at the Nanuet Post Office.)

Question # 3—We are going on vacation for two weeks, what should I do?

Answer—Don't let mail build up in your mailbox while you are away. This could be an easy clue to burglars that you are not at home. Notify the Post Office or your carrier to hold your mail while you are gone. Upon your return pick up the mail held at the post office. Regular delivery service will resume after you have picked up the mail held at the post office.

Question # 4—I get so much mail, occasionally I will find a piece on the ground when I go to take it in the house? Should I tell someone?

Answer—In recent years there has been a great increase in mail volume, especially in Third Class Mail. Many mailboxes are outdated or are too small to handle the present volume. Some mailboxes fail to protect the mail from the weather, while others are difficult to reach during curbside delivery. Take a look at your mailbox. Is it adequately protecting your precious mail? If your mailbox is adequate and the carrier repeatedly fails to secure your mail, then call your local post office and speak to the Supervisor of Postal Operations.

Question # 5—I'm 78 years old and I live alone. It is difficult for me to travel to the post office to obtain stamps. Can I buy them from the carrier?

Answer—Many of our postal patrons especially the elderly and the homebound are using our Stamps By Mail Service. The envelopes are available at your local post office or your mail carrier will be glad to get them for you. Just fill out the envelope, enclose a check and you can receive stamps on a regular basis without having to stop by the post office. Those who have used the service have expressed great satisfaction with it.

Question # 6—A large truck stalled in front of our curbside mailbox. It has been there for two days. Our carrier informed us that he is not required to dismount his postal vehicle to serve curbside boxes. Is this true?

Answer—Mail carriers request your cooperation in "training your visitors," service people and children not to block your curbside mailbox with cars, trucks or toys. For a host of safety reasons Postal Authorities do not want mailmen getting in and out of vehicles to serve curbside boxes. Explain the circumstances of your present situation involving the truck, I'm sure your carrier will understand and continue your mail delivery.

Question # 7—My mother is widowed and homebound and we live out of state. Could you tell me something about the Carrier Alert program.

Answer—The Carrier Alert Program was officially inaugurated in 1982 when then-Postmaster General William F. Bolger and Vince Sombrotto, President of the NALC signed a statement supporting an all volunteer effort to monitor elderly and disabled mail customers. The statement said in part that, "It has been customary for carriers to show particular consideration for customers on their routes whose health or advanced age required a little extra special attention."

When carriers note something that might signify illness or accident, they report it to a postal supervisor or another designated individual who in turn contacts the sponsoring local agency—the agency checks on the person—and if something's wrong, contact family, police or emergency services. To implement the program the NALC and USPS have joined forces with community service organizations as the American Red Cross, the United Way's First Call for Help and local Councils on Aging. Together they build a resource network that effectively keeps an eye on elderly and disabled patrons registered in the program. But letter carriers are the front line, the people who make the program work.

(The answer to the above question was supplied by the August 1990 issue of the *POSTAL RECORD*, a publication of the NALC for letter carriers and their families.)

Question # 8—What happens to a letter when it is sent to the Dead Letter Section?

Answer—Letters that are improperly addressed are "duds" and in large post offices the people who specialize in deciphering duds are called "nixie clerks" or "hard men." Letters that cannot be readdressed, or returned to the sender, end up in the dead-letter section of large post offices. Each year millions of letters and parcels meet that fate. Unclaimed cash found in these letters goes into postal revenues, likewise money from the sale of merchandise. Invariably the fault lies with the public: improper addressing, no return address, insecure packaging and wrapping.

Nixie clerks are like veteran detectives. They match wits with senders who address letters in Morse Code, in musical notes or numbers according to positions of letters in the alphabet. Occasionally these senders will use drawings, or chemical symbols, such as H_2otown for Watertown. Many of the "nixie clerks" troubles stem from misspelling and poor handwriting.

Articles spilled from containers often give employees their worst headaches. Poorly wrapped honey jars, an urn containing human ashes and bee hives are just a few of the items sent by mail. (The answer to question number eight was contained in a very interesting article written by Allan C. Fisher, Jr which appeared in the July 1954 issue of *National Geographic* magazine. It was entitled *EVERYONE'S SERVANT, THE POST OFFICE.*)

Question # 9—We used to receive our mail at 10:30 am, now we receive it at 1:30 pm. What happened?

Answer—Occasionally routes are readjusted due to growth and expansion of existing towns and neighborhood. The carrier's line of travel changes as does his arrival time because of the additions or deletions made to accommodate the new developments. This is done on an infrequent basis and probably accounts for the change in delivery time.

Question # 10—I'm a schoolteacher and I am frequently asked by my young students how a letter gets from one place to another. Does the post office give tours of its facilities?

Answer—Call your local postmaster and request a tour of their facility. The post office will be glad to accommodate your request. In most cases your class will be welcome to a guided tour and questions will be happily answered. There are also excellent videos available about how a letter is delivered. They are humorous and insightful. The post office often runs contests open to children. For example in October of 1990 your post office initiated a Stamp Design Contest with the theme Creatures of The Sea. The winning entry will receive a trip for four on an oceanic research vessel out of Norwalk, Connecticut. The contest is open to children 12 years old and under. Your carrier will be glad to assist you in arranging a tour for your class.

Question # 11—The town snowplow pushed snow in front of my mailbox. The mailman complains he can't get to the mailbox. Am I obligated to shovel all that snow?

Answer—The Postal Service request your cooperation in clearing a path to your mailbox. If you receive curbside delivery it is requested that you clear a path so that the mailman doesn't have to dismount the vehicle to serve you. Your mailman is not obligated to climb over mounds of snow to deliver your mail. Contact the town highway department if an excessive amount of snow is plowed in front of your mailbox.

Question # 12—We have two English Bulldogs, some of my neighbors complain they are pit bulls. When I was signing for a certified letter they bolted for the door and attacked the mailman. Luckily, he was not hurt as he defended himself with the mailbag and his spray. The mailman said we could have been sued for damages had he been bitten. Is this true?

Answer—Every year almost 3,000 carriers across the nation are bitten by dogs. A few are seriously maimed and spend a number of days in the hospital recovering from their wounds. The Postal Service takes the problem seriously and asks all dog owners to restrain their dogs by keeping them inside or securely leashed. When a carrier is bitten and requires medical attention the Postal Service will attempt to recoup the expenses involved in administering medical care and loss of the carrier's services.

Question # 13—Occasionally we have been receiving unsolicited sexually oriented advertisements in our mail. Is there any way to put a stop to this?

Answer—There are two postal forms you can use to stop delivery of unsolicited sexually oriented advertisements. The first form authorizes the Postal Service to issue an order prohibiting a specific mailer from sending you ads that you think are erotically arousing or sexually provocative. The second form authorizes the Postal Service to add your name to a list of people who do not want to receive sexually explicit ads from any mailer. To get the forms ask a window clerk at your post office for the *SOA Consumer Protection Packet.*

Question # 14—I received a letter in the mail telling me I could earn $400-$600 per month stuffing envelopes in my own home. I paid the $35.00 fee and all I received was a set of instructions on how to place ads. Isn't this mail fraud and what can I do about it?

Answer—Mail fraud is a scheme to get money or anything of value from you by offering a product, service, or investment opportunity that does not live up to its claims. Prosecutors must prove the claims were intentionally misrepresented and that the mails were used to carry out the scheme. As McGruff, the crime fighting dog says in *A CONSUMER'S GUIDE TO POSTAL CRIME PREVENTION* "Nobody would fall for fraud if it looked like fraud, right? So most of the time it looks like something else—a good deal, a business opportunity, a gift, or a chance to make a quick buck." Take envelope stuffing. This is the most common kind of work-at-home fraud. Typically, there is nothing to stuff… instead, you receive instructions to place ads like the one you responded to. Other schemes require you to make baby booties, Christmas wreaths, or other specialty products for which there is little or no market. Work-at-home schemes will not guarantee regular salaried employment. They will require you to invest your money before explaining how a plan works or before you are sent instructions. The work you are asked to do often continues the fraud by getting other victims involved. Always suspect any ad claiming you can earn unusually high income with little or no effort on your part.

(The answer to question # 14 was reprinted from *A CONSUMER'S GUIDE TO POSTAL CRIME PREVENTION* published with permission from The Postal Inspection Service.)

Question # 15—I live in a pretty tough neighborhood, occasionally a friend of mine will report a check is missing. It has happened several times now. What can we do?

Answer—The Postal Service delivers millions of checks, money orders, savings bonds and other valuable items everyday. It works hard to make sure your daily mail gets to you safe and sound, but we need your help.

1)   Make sure your mailbox is in good condition. Mailboxes in poor condition often expose mail to theft and bad weather.

2)   Collect mail promptly, especially checks and food coupons. Don't let mail build up. If you are not at home,

3)   Contact the issuing agency if you do not receive an expected check, food coupons, or other valuable mail.

4)   Never send cash or coins through the mail. Always send a check or money order.

5)   Notify your post office and mailers immediately if you change your address. Your local post office has Change of Address cards for this purpose.

Question # 16—The continual dependence on foreign oil points up the need for America to develop alternative sources of fuel. As the owner of the second largest fleet of vehicles in the U.S., what is the Post Office doing to reduce its consumption of foreign oil.

Answer—The Postal Service has been a leader in testing such alternative energy sources as compressed natural gas, propane, hydrogen, alcohol and electricity. Mark Kodama, a reporter for the *FEDERAL TIMES* reported, "that of all the alternative sources tested, compressed natural gas has been the most promising. About 300 vehicles now run on compressed natural gas and more are expected." The Persian Gulf crisis has quickened the Postal Service's interest in developing cheaper alternative sources of fuel.

Chapter XV

Postal Kid's News
Stories for Young Children and the Young at Heart.
Things to Do and Build.

Many of the people who work in the Postal Service are parents with children ranging from the very young to those who have completed their schooling and are embarking on new careers. When I first started writing I wrote many articles and stories for children. In this chapter I would like to share some of those stories with our readers.

If you would like to teach a young child how to swim or build a goldfish pond in your backyard, just follow directions. Maybe it's raining outside and your young tyke is restless. She or he might enjoy *BERNADINE OF NADAWAN*, an allegory about democracy. Perhaps you and your child could benefit from a little exercise, then *A KINDERGYM PROGRAM FOR THE HOME* could help.

Those interested in postal related activities might enjoy *A LETTER FROM OMAHA* or *COLLECTING FIRST DAY COVERS*, a hobby I share with my own children. Have you ever wanted to learn about how kids live in other countries? Then join the *USPS OLYMPIC PEN* PAL CLUB and you'll receive a writing kit. My daughter writes to a teenage girl from Australia and she says it's lots of fun and who knows? Maybe she'll meet her someday. And last but not least *TERRY THE TREE DETECTIVE* teaches us to preserve our environment so that future generations will thrive and prosper and know that we cared during our stewardship here on this good earth.

Teach Your Children to Swim

When you teach your child to swim, you are teaching a skill they can enjoy for a lifetime. Swimming is best taught in a placid body of water, preferably a pool or a lake. The parent who enjoys swimming will make the best teacher. All you need is patience, enthusiasm and a few swimming aids. The first is a back float, which is a polyurethane bubble with a belt running through it. It is belted at the chest. The second item, called a water ring is a plastic circular ring five inches in diameter.

In chest deep water ask the child to bend over and blow bubbles through the ring. Instruct her to blow through her nose and mouth at the same time. After repeating this a number of times, take the ring and wear it as a crown. Submerge, all the while blowing bubbles through your nose and mouth. She'll imitate you. After she has accomplished this, drop the ring to the bottom of the pool. Slowly reach down, blow bubbles all the while, and retrieve the water ring. The child will want to try it. Pretty soon she is learning how to breathe while in the water, an important step in basic water safety.

Have your child climb out with her legs dangling over the dock or pool edge. Ask her to extend her legs and point her toes like a ballet dancer and kick the water without bending her knees. She'll do this with enthusiasm. Now have her hold on to the side of the pool or dock and practice kicking.

Again ask her to climb out and watch you swim across the pool. Take a leisurely swim emphasizing good stroking and kicking technique. Ask the child to move her arms in a similar fashion. Now we are ready to put on the back float. Tighten it snugly at the chest area. Let the child experience the pleasure of floating. Tell her to kick her legs; that will bring her to a prone position. Now she is ready to paddle with her arms, kick her legs and direct her movements.

Your child is beginning to master her environment and will want to try these things again and again. Have her paddle out to an object, such as a rope or the other side of the pool. Encourage her efforts while accompanying her. It is only a matter of time and practice before you can remove the float. You will get an indication of readiness when you see her breathing [blowing bubbles] and accelerating with ease.

When she feels she is ready to try swimming without a float, have her swim a short distance to you. Gradually increase the distance until she swims it with confidence. Learning to swim will add immeasurably to your child's sense of growth and mastery while giving her an activity she can enjoy the rest of her life.

A Letter from Omaha

WANTED
Orphan, No Living Family
Good Chance of Injury or Death
Will Hire for Pony Express Rider
High Pay

In the 1860's this ad would often appear in Western newspapers. Poor kids 14 and 15 years of age supporting families would often hire on as Pony Express riders. Of course delivering the mail today isn't as dangerous as it was in the days of the Pony Express. I mean you don't have to worry about being attacked by a band of Indians on the war path, just an occasional dog bite here and there. Last year 3,000 carriers were bitten by dogs across the U.S.

Did you ever wonder how that letter you received from Omaha reached your home? Let's back up a little and follow that letter that Gina mailed to you from a Post Office in Omaha, Nebraska, 1500 miles from where you live. Just how did it get to your house in Nanuet, NY in three days. Here is a scenario that occurs 3 billion times each week. That's how many letters and parcels our Postal Service handles every seven days.

On a trip to her local Rockbottom store Gina remembers to mail a letter she had written to her friend, Francesca who lives in Nanuet, NY. She places it in the mailbox just before entering the store. Two hours later a mailman walking by the collection box clears it of mail and continues on his route. After completing his route, he returns to his office and brings all the outgoing mail to a dispatch clerk. These letters are separated, machine stamped into trays; postage stamped into bins. Bert, our clerk wheels the bin onto a Post Con (postal container) where it is placed into a truck for a trip to Omaha MPC (mail processing center).

Larry Jackson, the driver, reaches the MPC and backs up unto the loading dock. The MPC is a huge automated mailing facility with computers, optical scanners, conveyors, bar-coders and canceling machines. Sacks of mail are everywhere.

As we follow our letter it is speeding overhead on a conveyor and tossed into a sorting machine which separates it according to size. It is then cancelled (they are those squiggly black stripes you see over the stamp. That prevents the stamp from being re-used and it also tells you where the letter originated and the date it was sent.

Lisa Givens, sitting at an optical scanner notes the destination and zip code. She punches several keys on her computer and our letter resumes its trip on a conveyor which tosses it into New York bound mail. There it is dumped into a large canvas bag and placed on a skid (a rolling platform). Two hours later our letter along with thousands of other letters is wheeled into a truck bound for

Omaha Airport. Our letter leaves on flight 227 with a stopover in Chicago. It arrives in New York 12 hours later.

A clerk working at the Kennedy International Airport MPC notes the address and types out a barcode (those lines on the bottom the size of a pencil thin mustache) on the lower end of the envelope. They tell the optical scanners what town in N.Y, what route it is on, and the street where the house is located and even where it is on the street (third house on the right).

Our letter is now speeding overhead and tossed into a sack destined for the Suffern, NY MPC, the center for mail addressed to Rockland County. In the Suffern MPC our letter is angled off to a sack which contains mail for the Nanuet Post Office. On Sunday, a Nanuet mail carrier working alone from 2pm to 4pm picks up the mail for the Nanuet Post Office, breaks it down for the clerks to sort, then he leaves the office

Monday Morning

Barbara Hopper sorts our letter into Route 8. She places a tray on the case of Joe Sidoti, the regular mail carrier for the route. Joe cases it into its street address. After casing all his mail for the day, Joe consolidates the bundles of mail and places our letter into the Grandview Relay bag where John Clinton, the relay man will place it in storage at the relay box on Grandview Avenue.

Joe reaches the box at 11:45am after walking 3 miles of his route. He places the letter into the mailbox at 12 Apollo Drive at 12:15pm and continues on his way.

Francesca goes to the mailbox after school and smiles as she notes the return address. After a 1,500 mile trip the letter has reached its destination. In 1861 it would have cost $5.00 and it would have taken three weeks to a month to reach its destination. Not bad for thirty nine cents, is it?

TOM RILEY

Terry, the Tree Detective

My name is Terry and I'm a tree detective. Reading a tree is like reading a book. In fact *WE DELIVER* was once a tree before it was processed into a book. Homes, furniture, boats, magazines and many other items are all by-products of trees. Trees give us the air we breathe, prevent erosion and offer shade to the weary traveler. Trees are among man's best friend.

My uncle Dave is a forest ranger and he taught me how to become a tree detective. He showed me how to read the rings of a cross-section of a tree to learn about it's life history. Let's take a walk and play detective. I know where two trees have been cut down recently. Let's read them and learn their story.

Trees live interesting lives just like people. By seeing a cross-section of a tree you can play detective and tell others about their lives. You can tell about droughts, fires, years of bug infestation, hard times, happy times, years of struggle, disease and recovery, periods of prosperity and good nutrition or years of poor health. A tree is almost like a person. It's a living thing like you and me and it struggles to live wherever it finds itself.

Let's look at the rings of that tree which once grew on the rocky soil on the side of that hill. By counting the rings we learn that it is thirty eight years old. The rings on one side are thicker for at least five years. That means this rock was leaning against it while it was a sapling. The side away from the rock grew thick and strong and eventually moved the rock away. This dark section on the fifteenth ring shows that a forest fire raged and almost destroyed the tree, but we had good growth in its seventeenth year. When it was twenty we notice thin rings for at least five years. That means a series of cold winters or drought. We have another series of thin rings again at thirty years of age. These are very thin and point to an infestation of some sort. If you remember we had a caterpillar epidemic about eight years ago. They denuded the tree of leaves and severely threatened it. If you look at the soil it is rocky and claylike. This rock near the tree served a useful purpose it preserved water and prevented evaporation. Let's walk to the stump of a larger pine which was recently cut down. A tree can grow up rich too. We can see that this tree grew up in rich loamy soil. This provided a happy environment for the tree to prosper and grow. There is that forest fire ring we saw before, but there is no infestation at thirty years of age. This tree was forty eight years old when it was cut down.

Do you see that tree over there? That's a great help to mankind. It's called a Taxus Yew and the bark of that tree contains an ingredient that has saved the lives of thousands of women suffering from ovarian cancer. There aren't too many Taxus Yews around so each one is to be treasured and cared for so that someday when it is cut down lives can be saved.

When I think about what is happening to the destruction of our rain forest all over the world, it saddens me a little. A tree that provides the oxygen we breathe, a home for birds and shade for the weary traveler is cut down to provide land for farming. The decade-long droughts that have occurred in Ethiopia should have taught us a lesson. Rain forest once covered that land but thousands of years of clearing land for farming has turn that country into a near desert. Today only seven percent of the land contains trees. Trees hold the land together, prevent erosion and flooding.

A country can turn into a desert if it doesn't care for its life giving trees. Trees have a story to tell. Care for a tree and it'll have a happy ending.

Collecting First Day Covers

A First Day Cover is a new issue of a stamp placed on an envelope and mailed from a designated post office to collectors all over the world. After the first day has past, post offices all over the United States can now sell that stamp to customers. The designated post office is usually the birthplace or locale of the event or person being honored. One of my favorite covers is an Express Mail stamped envelope sent aloft on the Challenger Space Shuttle. While whirling around the earth the cargo bay doors were open to the sun and the cover was exposed to rays from outer space. The Challenger returned to Edwards Air Force Base in California, (I had been stationed there while in the Air Force). Tragically, years later that same Challenger space craft exploded after take-off killing seven astronauts. To me that First Day Cover is a memorial and a historical reminder of the great events of American history.

First day Covers offer a panorama of Americana. Personalities, inventions, extraordinary leaders in many different fields and everyday events such as as love, family unity, education and work are celebrated by renowned engravers for their contribution to American life. You can have the Covers addressed to you or unaddressed.

Information on collecting First day Covers are available at your local post office or you can contact the Postal Commemorative Society in Norwalk, Connecticut. On the average a First Day Cover will cost from $1.50 to $2.50. Collecting First Day Covers is an informative and rewarding hobby for young and old alike. I enjoy collecting First Day Covers for the beauty of the engraving on the envelope which accompanies the stamp and for the wealth of information about the event being celebrated. First Day Covers increase in value and satisfaction with each new issue.

A Kindergym Program for the Home

In an era of two family wage earners, postal parents want the time spent with their children to be quality time. This desire and a concern for good health and fitness can be satisfied through Kindergym, a regimen of exercises to do at home that children from two to eight years old will enjoy. All that is needed is an open space (a carpeted living room or recreation room is ideal), a jump rope and a Hula-Hoop.

One of the best times to interest your children in Kindergym would be about forty-five minutes after the family has eaten supper. Clear an area about ten feet by fifteen feet for your exercise area. Standing before you will be your two-to-six-old, full of boundless energy and eager to show off his or her physical prowess. Begin the session with a song that points to and acts out its phrases.

"Head, shoulders, knees and toes
Knees and toes
Head, shoulders, knees and toes
Head, shoulders, knees and toes
Eyes, ears, mouth and nose"

Then jog in place for one minute. After a short rest, begin arm circles, forward and backward. Now do toe touches. Rest, for thirty seconds. Our next exercise will be torso rotations-rotating the upper torso from the waist in a circular motion.

Now take a sitting position on the carpet. Have your child face you with heels touching and arms extended, grasping each other's hands. Sing "Row, Row, Row Your Boat," varying the tempo while you row with your imaginary oars. End with a thirty-second rest, lying on your backs.

From this position, swing both legs up over the head with an effort at touching the floor with your toes. Hold fifteen seconds, then begin again. Rest. Your next exercise will be bicycle kicks.

Support your lower back, then move your legs in a cycling fashion. Rest. Now roll over on your stomach, and do push-ups.

After resting thirty seconds, get up and jog around your house or apartment for three minutes. As time goes by, extend the time you jog to realize the full benefit of aerobic exercise.

Use your Hula-Hoop and jump-rope in the conventional manner. Each will take practice to perfect. Your jump rope can also be used in lieu of a balance beam. Spread it out straight and walk its length. Balance is important for coordination.

At each session you can introduce your favorite activity or expand on one the children enjoy. End with a one minute run.

You and your children will enjoy the benefits of physical exercise and the fun of a shared activity. You will also be training your child at an early age the importance of keeping fit. Talking with your child about getting enough rest and good nutrition for a healthy lifestyle will round out your Kindergym Program for the Home.

Things to Do: Build a Goldfish Pond

Building a goldfish pond is a project that will provide hours of fun and cost less than $28.00. All you need is a spade or shovel, a tarp liner, a few decorative blocks and, of course, the fish. Add water, a few aquatic plants, and a dash of fish food and nature will take care of the rest.

Your goldfish pond will be a magnet for curious children, neighbors and friends who stop by for a visit. Within weeks you'll notice those little feeder goldfish have grown into healthy robust adults-not bad when you can get seven for a dollar at your local pet store. In my pond, goldfish, guppies and catfish live happily together.

Children enjoy the darting antics and ravenous appetites of tropical fish, the secret nefarious travels of catfish and the flaring multicolored tail of the male guppy. Birds are attracted to the water supply, while dogs and cats stare at the fish and sometimes drink water from the pond. Contrary to what you may think, cats offer no threat to the fish. Our neighbor's cat laps water while the fish playfully dart near his tongue.

The hardest part of the whole project will be digging the pond. My pond measures two feet by three feet and is twenty-two inches deep. The secret to lively and healthy fish lies in the depth of the pond. Summer sun will make your pond a hot tub if the fish have no cooling depth to descend to. A minimum of eighteen inches is sufficient depth; twenty four inches is preferable. If you want to build a larger pond and keep your goldfish outside all year round your minimum depth will have to be three feet. Goldfish, but not guppies can weather the winter in an ice-covered pond. In areas where the winter temperature gets very cold, you'll have to bring your fish indoors around the middle of October. Guppies should be brought indoors in mid-September.

After you have dug your pond, you will be ready to install the liner. Take a few precautions with this step. Sometimes you'll run into tree or bush roots while digging. You can use cardboard or wood to prevent the roots from puncturing your liner. In my pond I placed cardboard all around the sides, then form-fitted my tarp liner over the cardboard. I purchased my tarp liner in a garden nursery for $7.50.

Once my tarp liner-a waterproof plasticized covering-was form fitted over the cardboard, all that was left to be done was to cover the rough edges of the liner with decorative blocks. Eight blocks for eighty five cents apiece gave the pond a neat appearance and acted as a barrier to prevent debris from falling into the pond. They also provided a place from which I can observe the fish.

A few aquatic plants and pebbles scattered about the bottom of the pond make a natural setting for your fish. If you should forget the daily feeding, the fish will thrive on the aquatic plants.

Add water, and let it settle for 12 hours to dissipate any chlorine. Add your new fish, still in the waterproof bag in which you brought them home from the pet store. Before releasing them from the bag, make sure they've become acclimatized to the surrounding water temperature. Now, just open the bag and you've created a new environment in your backyard.

The Olympic Penpal Club

When you think of the U.S. Postal Service you probably picture a letter carrier delivering mail to your house. But did you know the Postal Service is sponsoring the Olympic Pen Pal Club. Kids from all over the world are writing letters to each other. My daughter writes to a teenage girl from Australia. This helps her to collect the beautiful stamps which Australia issues and she learns a lot about life in Australia. Who knows maybe someday we will visit her Pen Pal. For further information about how to join the Olympic Pen Pal Club and receive their Pen Pal Kit write to:

USPS OLYMPIC PEN PAL CLUB
PO BOX 9419
GAITHERSBURG, MD 20898-9419

Postal Facts
Surprising Facts About the U.S. Postal Service.

* America's largest civilian employer with nearly three quarters of a million employees.

* If listed in the "Fortune 500," the Postal Service would be the nation's ninth largest corporation (annual revenues $43 billion)

* Makes 117 million house calls, six days a week.

* Delivers 40 percent of the world's mail volume.
* Suggestions received per year for commemorative stamps: 30,000. Number issued: 30 to 40.

Mail Volume

The USPS collects, processes and delivers nearly 550 million pieces of mail per day.

Total mail—166.3 billion pieces, up 2.9 percent over 1990.

First-Class Mail—89.3 billion pieces, 53.7 percent of the total volume, up 4 percent.

Second-Class—10.7 billion pieces, 6.4 percent of total volume, up 1.5 percent.

Third-Class—63.7 billion pieces, 38.3 percent of total volume, up, up 1.5 percent

Fourth-Class—0.66 billion pieces, 0.4 percent of total volume, up 5.9 percent.

International—0.80 billion pieces, 0.5 percent of total volume, up 10.3 percent.

Average Daily Mail volume—547 million pieces.

Operations

Forty-nine percent of all letter mail was handled on automated equipment in Fiscal Year 1990, up from 42 percent in the previous year.

Automated mail handling is more than 10 times faster than manual operations. It cost $40.00 to process 1,000 letters by manual sorting and $18.00 by mechanized equipment, but only $4.00 by automation.

In the next two years, total automated equipment deployed will grow more than 2,500 to about 67,000-major steps toward the 1995 goal of 10,000. By 1995, the Postal Service hopes this equipment and cooperative programs with mailers will place a bar code on virtually all mail.

Cost per delivery point in Fiscal Year 1990 was $158 for door, $112 for curbside and $95 for centralized delivery.

Employees

Total Career Employees—1990	760,668
(down 30,000 from May 1989)	
Headquarters	2,291
Headquarters Field Support Unit	5,691
Regional Offices	542
Inspection Service (Field)	4,259
Postmasters	26,995
Supervisors	43,458
Prof. /Admin. /Tech	9,793
Clerks	290,380
Motor Vehicle Operators	7,308
Mail Handlers	51,123
Rural Carriers and Subs.	
on Vacant Routes	42,252
Special Delivery Messengers	2,012
Bldg. and Equip. Maintenance	33,323
Vehicle Maintenance	4,874
Nurses	286
City Letter Carriers	236,081

Non-Career Employees

Casuals	26,829
Non-Bargaining Temporaries	414
Rural Subs/RCA/RCR/AUX	43,373
Postmaster Relief Replacements	11,979

Post Offices, Stations, Branches and Routes

Total	40,067
Post Offices	28,959
Classified Stations and Branches	5,008
Contract Stations and Branches	4,397
Community Post Offices	1,703
Rural Deliveries	20.7 million
Possible City Deliveries	77.9 million
Post Office Boxes	17.9 million

Corporate Strategic Goals

Enhance Customer Satisfaction

*   Opened Postal Business Centers throughout the country to offer information and assistance to small and medium-sized business mailers.
*   Improved retail convenience by expanding hours of service, adding self—service vending equipment and by selling stamps by mail, phone and on consignment to local businesses.

Keep Costs Below Inflation

*   Costs increased two percentage points less than inflation.
*   Increased productivity by 3.1 percent, 10 times the historic average.
*   Accelerated automation program—more than 3,000 pieces of equipment slated for deployment in the next two years.

Increase Employee Commitment

*   Continued Employee Involvement/Quality of Work Life process with 6,500 work teams
*   Became Corporate sponsor for 1992 Olympic Games.

New Postmaster General Takes Office July 6th, 1992

Postmaster General Marvin Runyon took office on July 6th, 1992. He promises to revamp the organizational structure of the Postal Service so that it is more responsive to customer needs. He stressed his commitment to competitiveness and rate stabilization. To accomplish these goals he has set 30 day, 60 day and 90 day targets for a transformation into a leaner and stronger Postal Service.

Postmaster Runyon comes from a 37 year career as a CEO in the automotive industry. He recently completed tenure as head of the Tennessee Valley Authority where he implemented a marked reduction in personnel which made the TVA more efficient and profitable. "Very soon, the Postal service will have in place the right structure, the right processes, and the right attitude to serve you. First, we will maintain stable rates through at least 1994. Second, we will make automated mail the lowest cost letter mail, and delivery point bar-coding will be a central feature in this savings to the public. Third, we will revisit our entire rate structure and processes to make our products and prices simpler and more user-friendly. Customer needs aren't static; they are always evolving and changing, and we intend to increase your satisfaction with us, now and in the future."

As we go to press Postmaster Runyon has begun the first phase of reducing the management structure of the Postal Service. He has offered early retirement incentives which he hopes will result in a reduction of 40,000 fewer Postal employees. The restructuring currently underway will be completed in November. It will cut costs and reduce layers of bureaucracy to enable employees to be more responsive to customer needs.

How to Apply for
Postal Service Employment

An applicant for a Postal Service job must pass a written examination, meet minimum age requirements, and be a U.S. citizen. The minimum age is 18, but a high school graduate may begin work at 16 if the job is not hazardous and does not require driving a motor vehicle. Applicants for Postal Service jobs are hired on the basis of their examination scores.

If you are interested in taking the test for postal employment stop by your local post office and ask the window clerk when the exam will be given. If an examination is scheduled in the near future she will hand you an application. Examinations for most jobs include a written test that checks a person's vocabulary and reading ability as well as their aptitude for remembering addresses. Five points are added to the score of honorably discharged veterans, and ten points are added to the score of a veteran wounded in combat or disabled. The appointing officer chooses an applicant for an open job from the results of their test score.

New employees are trained on the job by supervisors and other experienced employees. *Training ranges from a few days to several months, depending on the job. Postal workers are classified as casual, part-time flexible, part-time regular, or full time. Casuals workers are not career employees, but are hired to help handle the large amounts of mail during the Christmas season and for other short-term assignments. Part-time flexible employees, although they have career status, do not have a regular work schedule but replace absent workers or help with extra workloads as the need arises. Part-time regulars have a set work schedule-for example, 6 hours a day. Carriers, clerks, and mail handlers may start as part-time flexible workers and move into full-time jobs according to their seniority as vacancies occur.

Postal workers can advance to better paying jobs by learning new skills. Training programs are available. Also, employees can get preferred assignments, such as a more desirable delivery route, as their seniority increases. When an opening occurs, eligible employees may submit written requests called "bids" for assignment to the vacancy. The bidder who has the qualifications and the most seniority gets the job.

There are hundreds of different employment opportunities in the U.S. Postal Service. The Postal Service employs workers in a variety of supervisory, administrative, and clerical jobs. Lawyers, engineers, physicians, accountants, computer specialists, advertising specialists are just a few of the job opportunities available.

Postmasters and mail supervisors are responsible for the day-to-day operations of the post office. They supervise clerks and carriers, hire and train employees and set up their work schedule. They measure mail volume and ensure that the mail is delivered in a safe and prompt manner. They handle customer complaints and participate in the Employee Involvement Program to improve the quality of work life in their offices. They perform numerous other duties to ensure that their office maintains high standards of quality and service in the delivery of mail.

* The Letter Carrier Academy provides all new employees with several days of classroom orientation followed by on the job instruction.

Glossary of U.S. Postal Terms

AIR MAIL—Provides faster service than first-class from the United States to all other countries except Canada. Within the United States and Canada air service has been merged with first-class.

CERTIFIED MAIL—Proof of delivery is provided to the sender.

COLLECT-ON-DELIVERY—(COD) Addressee pays for value of merchandise he has ordered, plus shipping charges and COD fee upon delivery.

EXPRESS MAIL—Provides a premium overnight service between hundreds of U.S. cities and several foreign countries. Up to 40 pounds (10kg) of letters, reports, magnetic tapes, merchandise, and other mail items can be dispatched in the distinctive Express Mail pouches.

FIRST-CLASS MAIL—Letters, post cards, all matter wholly or partially in writing, and all matter sealed or otherwise closed against postal inspection.

FOURTH-CLASS MAIL-(PARCEL POST)—Merchandise, printed matter, mailable live animals, and all other matter not included in first-, second-, or third-class mail.

INSURED MAIL—A service whereby postal customers who have paid a special fee in advance may obtain payment for loss of, or damage to, mail.

MAILGRAM—A written message transmitted electronically by Western Union to a distant post office and delivered by the U.S. Post Office.

MONEY ORDERS—A safe way to send money through the mail. Money orders are sold in all post offices. They are widely accepted and fully negotiable.

PRIORITY MAIL—First-Class items weighing more than 13 ounces (404 grams) and air mail exceeding 10 ounces (311 grams) are in this class. Often called air parcel post, priority mail is carried by air whenever it will expedite delivery.

REGISTERED MAIL—Offers a high degree of security for negotiable documents, jewelry, cash, and other valuables.

SECOND-CLASS MAIL—All newspapers, magazines, and other periodicals issued at stated intervals. A second-class permit must be obtained from your postmaster.

SPECIAL DELIVERY—Available where there is city carrier service and within one mile (0.6km) radius of small post offices. In addition to delivery by a messenger, special Glossary of U.S. Postal Terms delivery parcel post is carried on preferential surface transportation.

SPECIAL HANDLING—Qualifies parcel post for preferential surface transportation.

THIRD-CLASS MAIL—Usually advertising circulars, printed matter, pamphlets, and merchandise weighing less than 16 ounces (498 grams). Consult your postmaster for the category of third-class mail best suited for your needs.

(The Glossary of U.S. Postal Terms was reprinted from the *ENCYCLOPEDIA AMERICANA,* 1990 international edition—Grolier Incorporated. Volume 22, page 457.)

Postmaster Generals of the United States

Name	Took Office	Under President
Benjamin Franklin	1775	#
Richard Bache	1776	##
Ebenezer Hazard	1782	*
Samuel Osgood	1789	Washington
Timothy Pickering	1791	Washington
Joseph Habersham	1785	Washington
		J. Adams
		Jefferson
Gideon Granger	1801	Jefferson
		Madison
Return Meigs, Jr.	1814	Madison
		Monroe
John McLean	1823	Monroe
		J.Q. Adams
		Jackson
William T. Barry	1829	Jackson
Amos Kendall	1835	Jackson
		Van Buren
John M. Niles	1840	Van Buren
Francis Granger	1841	W.H. Harrison
		Tyler
Charles A. Wickliffe	1841	Tyler
Cave Johnson	1845	Polk
Jacob Collamer	1849	Taylor
Nathan K. Hall	1850	Fillmore

Sam D. Hubbard	1852	Fillmore
James Campbell	1853	Pierce
Aaron V. Brown	1857	Buchanan
Joseph Holt	1859	Buchanan
Horatio King	1861	Buchanan
Lincoln		
Montgomery Blair	1861	Lincoln
William Dennison	1864	Lincoln
A. Johnson		
Alexander W. Randall	1866	A. Johnson
John A.J. Creswell	1869	Grant
James W. Marshall	1874	Grant
Marshall Jewell	1874	Grant
James N. Tyner	1876	Grant
David M. Key	1877	Hayes
Horace Maynard	1880	Hayes
Thomas L. James	1881	Garfield
Arthur		
Timothy O. Howe	1881	Arthur
Walter Q. Gresham	1883	Arthur
Frank Hatton	1884	Arthur
William F. Vilas	1885	Cleveland
Don M. Dickinson	1888	Cleveland
John Wanamaker	1889	B. Harrison
Wilson S. Bissell	1893	Cleveland
William L. Wilson	1895	Cleveland
James Gary	1897	McKinley
Charles E. Smith	1898	McKinley
T. Roosevelt		
Henry C. Payne	1902	T. Roosevelt
Robert J. Wynne	1904	T. Roosevelt
George B. Cortelyou	1905	T. Roosevelt
George von L. Meyer	1907	T. Roosevelt

Frank H. Hitchcock	1909	Taft
Albert S. Burleson	1913	Wilson
Will Hays	1921	Harding
Hubert Work	1922	Harding
Harry S. New	1923	Harding
Coolidge		
Hoover		
Walter F. Brown	1929	Hoover
James A. Farley	1933	F.D. Roosevelt
Frank C. Walker	1940	F.D. Roosevelt
Truman		
Robert E. Hannegan	1945	Truman
Jesse M. Donaldson	1947	Truman
Arthur E. Summerfield	1953	Eisenhower
J. Edward Day	1961	Kennedy
John A. Gronouski	1963	Kennedy/L.B. Johnson
Lawrence F. O'Brien	1965	L.B. Johnson
W. Marvin Watson	1968	L.B. Johnson
Winton M. Blount	1969	Nixon
Elmer T. Klassen	1972	-
Benjamin F. Bailar	1975	-
William F. Bolger	1978	-
Paul N. Carlin	1985	-
Albert V. Casey	1986	-
Preston R. Tisch	1986	-
AnthonV M. Frank	1988	-
Marvin Runyon	1992	-

\#   Served under the Continental Congress
\#\#   Served under the Congress of The Conferation
-    Since 1971, the Postmaster General has been appointed by the Board of Governors of the U.S. Postal Service instead of the President.

Bibliography

"Pastimes; Stamps," by Barth Healey, April 1, 1990. Copyright by the *New York Times Company*. Reprinted by permission.

Publication 100, *History of the U.S. Postal Service 1775-1984* Speech on Postal History by former Postmaster General Benjamin Bailar at Monmouth College, Monmouth, Illinois on October 16, 1975

Did You Know—Trivia and Postal Lore—permission granted by Rita L. Moroney, Researcher/Administrator/Historian U.S. Postal Service

Democratic Vistas: Post Offices and Public Art in the New Deal by Marlene Parks and Gerald Markowitz © 1984 by Temple University. Reprinted by permission of *Temple University Press*

Carrier Exploits On and Off the Job and EARTH: Handle with Care: Reprinted with permission from *THE POSTAL RECORD*, a publication of National Association of Letter Carriers
Stamps reprinted with permission by H.E. Harris & Co., Portsmouth, New Hampshire
Amazing But True Stories by Doug Storer and *Soliloquy of a Postage Stamp*

"Remembering '70: Workers Risk It All in Historic Strike" from March 26, 1990 issue of *Federal Times* and "Inspectors' *Crime*

Labs Mark 50th Anniversary" in the March 5, 1990 issue of *Federal Times.* Reprint Courtesy of *Federal Times* Copyright by *Times Journal Company*, Springfield, Virginia

Live Televised Debate: "*ABC News, Nightline*" on March 16th 1990 involving Postmaster General Anthony M. Frank, Ted Koppel, James Miller, Moe Biller and Ralph Nader

"*The Pony Express*" by Rowe Findley July 1980 Edition of *National Geographic Magazine* reprinted by permission of the National Geographic Society

"*Meet Our Postmaster General, Anthony M. Frank*" Spring 1988 edition of *POSTAL LIFE*, a magazine for postal employees and their families. Reprinted by permission from *POSTAL LIFE.*

"*Automation 1990*" permission granted to reprint portions of the *Northeast Regional Bulletin* article on Automation, July 1990 edition.

"*The Postal Inspection Service*" information supplied by Paul M. Griffo, Senior Information Specialist of The Postal Inspection Service from Semi-Annual Report 1990. "*A Consumer Guide to Postal Crime Prevention*" is published by The United States Postal Inspection Service

Information on the early history of the postal service worldwide available from *Encyclopedia Britannica, The Guinness Book of Stamps, Facts and Feats* by James MacKay, *Collier's Encyclopedia*, and the *World Book Encyclopedia*

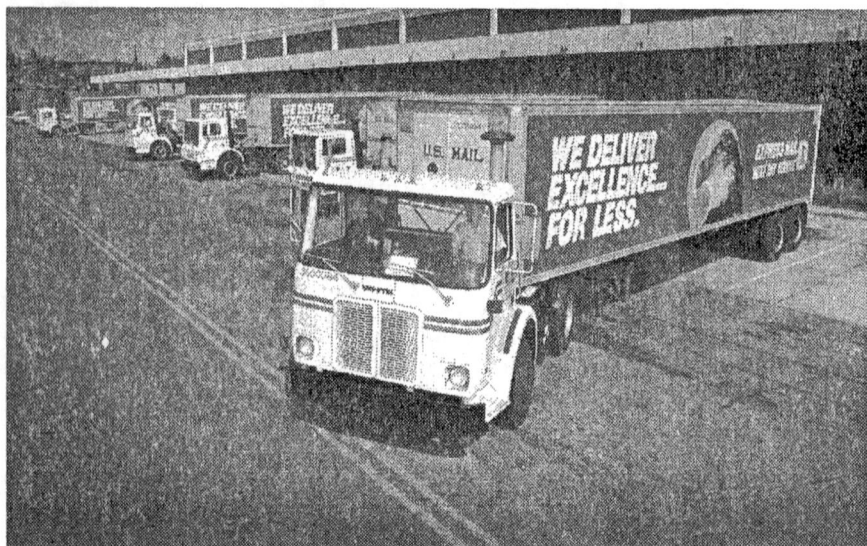

About the Author

Tom Riley is a retired mail carrier with 27 years seniority at the Nanuet, NY Post Office. He was born in the Bronx in 1941. One of 12 children he was sent along with his brothers and sisters to Happy Valley School in Pomona, NY. when his mother took ill. "We loved it there, fields and woods to roam in and 3 square meals a day. All the sports you could think of and work everyday after school. We grew our own vegetables, milked cows, fixed roads or cleaned the gym for a dance after a hard fought basketball game against a local rival." Tom wrote a book about his experiences at Happy Valley and during research uncovered previously unpublished material about the "orphan trains" of the 1800's. Tom is the author of *ORPHAN TRAIN RIDERS*, Volume 1 and 2, *THE SAGA OF JOHNNY EDEN and WE DELIVER*

Tom enlisted in the Air Force at 17 and served almost 4 years as a photographer. He attended LIU and Iona College under the G.I. Bill. Mr. Riley lives in New City, NY with his wife, Crucy, a guidance counselor in the Mt. Vernon School System and his two daughters, Gina and Bernadette.

The Carriers of the Nanuet Post Office pose for a picture after winning a National Safety Award for Safe Driving.

Heritage Books by the author:

Andrew Horace Burke
A Man for All Seasons: The Incredible Story of an Orphan Train Rider
and Civil War Drummer Boy Who Grew Up to Become
the Governor of North Dakota

Happy Valley School: A History and Remembrance

Orphan Train Riders: A Brief History of the Orphan Train Era (1854–1929)
with Entrance Records from the American Female Guardian
Society's Home for the Friendless in New York
Volume One

Orphan Train Riders: Entrance Records from the
American Female Guardian Society's Home
for the Friendless in New York
Volume Two

The Orphan Train to Destiny

We Deliver: A Chronicle of the Deeds Performed by the
Men and Women of the U.S. Postal Service

www.ingramcontent.com/pod-product-compliance
Lightning Source LLC
Chambersburg PA
CBHW070249290326
41930CB00041B/2313